Joint Workshop on Language Technology for Closely Related Languages, Varieties and Dialects 2015

International Conference on Recent Advances in Natural Language Processing 2015

Hissar, Bulgaria
10 September 2015

ISBN: 978-1-5108-1784-5

Printed from e-media with permission by:

Curran Associates, Inc.
57 Morehouse Lane
Red Hook, NY 12571

Some format issues inherent in the e-media version may also appear in this print version.

Printed by Curran Associates, Inc. (2015)

For permission requests, please contact the Association for Computational Linguistics at the address below.

Association for Computational Linguistics
209 N. Eighth Street
Stroudsburg, Pennsylvania 18360

Phone: 1-570-476-8006
Fax: 1-570-476-0860

acl@aclweb.org

Additional copies of this publication are available from:

Curran Associates, Inc.
57 Morehouse Lane
Red Hook, NY 12571 USA
Phone: 845-758-0400
Fax: 845-758-2634
Email: curran@proceedings.com
Web: www.proceedings.com

Introduction

A large number of closely related language varieties and dialects are in daily use, not only as spoken colloquial languages but also in some written media, e.g., in SMS, chats, and social networks. Language resources for these varieties and dialects are sparse and building them could be very labor intensive. Yet, these efforts can often be reduced by making use of pre-existing resources and tools for related, resource-richer languages.

Examples of closely-related language varieties include the different variants of Spanish in Latin America, the Arabic dialects in North Africa and the Middle East, German in Germany, Austria and Switzerland, French in France and in Belgium, etc. Examples of pairs of related languages include Swedish-Norwegian, Bulgarian-Macedonian, Serbian-Bosnian, Spanish-Catalan, Russian-Ukrainian, Irish-Gaelic Scottish, Malay-Indonesian, Turkish–Azerbaijani, Mandarin-Cantonese, Hindi–Urdu, etc.

Recent interest in language resources and technology for closely related languages, varieties and dialects has led to previous editions of the LT4CloseLang workshop at RANLP2013 and EMNLP2014, and of the VarDial workshop at COLING2014. Both the LT4CloseLang and the VarDial workshops have attracted a lot of research interest, which indicated that there was need for further activities. Thus, this year we decided to join forces between these two workshops and to organize a joint workshop, LT4VarDial, aiming to bring together researchers interested in building language resources for language varieties or dialects and in creating language technology that makes use of language closeness and exploits existing resources in a related language or a language variant.

As part of the workshop, we organized the second edition of the DSL Shared Task on Discriminating between Similar Languages. The first edition was held in conjunction with VarDial, aiming to distinguish between closely related languages and language varieties, thus filling the research gap in fine-grained language identification, which was previously perceived as a solved task. Yet, DSL remains a challenge for state-of-the-art language identification. The attention received from the research community and the feedback provided by the participants of the first edition motivated us to organize this Second DSL Shared Task, where we made two important changes compared to the first edition. First, in order to simulate a real-world language identification scenario, we included in the testing dataset some languages that were not present in the training dataset. Moreover, we included a second test set, where we substituted the named entities with placeholders to make the task more challenging and less dependent on the text topic and domain.

A total of 24 teams subscribed to participate in the shared task, 10 of them submitted official runs, and 8 of the latter also wrote system description papers. These numbers represent a slight increase in participation compared to the 2014 edition, which attracted 22 teams, 8 submissions, and 5 system description papers.

Overall, 12 papers are published in this volume. Nine papers were about the DSL shared task (8 system descriptions and the shared task overview), and three regular workshop papers.

Given the above numbers, we consider the workshop a success, and we take the opportunity to thank the LT4VarDial program committee for their professional and thorough reviews, and the DSL Shared Task participants for the valuable feedback and discussions. We further thank our invited speakers and our panelists for sharing with us their thought-provoking opinions on topics of interest to the workshop.

The workshop organizers: *Preslav Nakov, Marcos Zampieri, Petya Osenova, Liling Tan, Cristina Vertan, Nikola Ljubešić, and Jörg Tiedemann*

Workshop Organizers

Preslav Nakov, Qatar Computing Research Institute, HBKU (Qatar)
Marcos Zampieri, Saarland University and DFKI (Germany)
Petya Osenova, Bulgarian Academy of Sciences (Bulgaria)
Liling Tan, Saarland University (Germany)
Cristina Vertan, University of Hamburg (Germany)
Nikola Ljubešić, University of Zagreb (Croatia)
Jörg Tiedemann, University of Uppsala (Sweden)

DSL Shared Task Organizers

Liling Tan, Saarland University (Germany)
Marcos Zampieri, Saarland University and DFKI (Germany)
Nikola Ljubešić, University of Zagreb (Croatia)
Jörg Tiedemann, University of Uppsala (Sweden)
Preslav Nakov, Qatar Computing Research Institute, HBKU (Qatar)

Program Committee

Željko Agić (University of Copenhagen, Denmark)
Laura Alonso y Alemany (Univeristy of Cordoba, Argentina)
Jorge Baptista (University of Algarve and INESC-ID, Portugal)
Eckhard Bick (University of Southern Denmark)
Francis Bond (Nanyang Technological University, Singapore)
Aoife Cahill (Educational Testing Service, United States)
José Castaño (University of Buenos Aires, Argentina)
Paul Cook (University of New Brunswick, Canada)
Marta Costa-Jussà (Institute for Infocomm Research, Singapore)
Liviu Dinu (University of Bucarest, Romania)
Stefanie Dipper (Ruhr University Bochum, Germany)
Sascha Diwersy (University of Cologne, Germany)
Tomaž Erjavec (Jozef Stefan Institute, Slovenia)
Mikel L. Forcada (Universitat d'Alacant, Spain)
Maria Gavrilidou (ILSP, Greece)
Binyam Gebrekidan Gebre (Max Planck Institute for Psycholinguistics, Holland)
Nizar Habash (Columbia University, USA)
Barry Haddow (University of Edinburgh, UK)
Chu-Ren Huang (Hong Kong Polytechnic University, Hong Kong)
Nitin Indurkhya (University of New South Wales, Australia)
Jeremy Jancsary (Nuance Communications, Austria)
Marco Lui (University of Melbourne, Australia)
Vladislav Kuboň (Charles University Prague, Czech Republic)
Shervin Malmasi (Macquarie University, Australia)
Graham Neubig (Nara Institute of Science and Technology, Japan)
John Nerbonne (University of Groningen, Netherlands)
Kemal Oflazer (Carnegie-Mellon University, Qatar)
Maciej Ogrodniczuk (IPAN, Polish Academy of Sciences, Poland)
Santanu Pal (Saarland University, Germany)

Reinhard Rapp (University of Mainz, Germany and University of Aix-Marseille, France)
Laurent Romary (INRIA, France)
Kevin Scanell (Saint Louis University, USA)
Yves Scherrer (University of Geneva, Switzerland)
Serge Sharoff (University of Leeds, United Kingdom)
Kiril Simov (Bulgarian Academy of Sciences, Bulgaria)
Milena Slavcheva (Bulgarian Academy of Sciences)
Marko Tadić (University of Zagreb, Croatia)
Elke Teich (Saarland University, Germany)
Joel Tetreault (Yahoo! Labs, USA)
Francis Tyers (UiT Norgga árktalaš universitehta, Norway)
Duško Vitas (University of Belgrade, Serbia)
Pidong Wang (National University of Singapore, Singapore)
Taro Watanabe (NICT, Japan)

Additional Reviewers

Maja Miličević
Tanja Samardžić

Invited Speakers

Leon Derczynski (Sheffield University, UK)
Eckhard Bick (University of Southern Denmark, Denmark)

Panelists

Marcos Zampieri (Saarland University and DFKI, Germany) – moderator
Cyril Goutte (National Research Council, Canada)
Marc Franco-Salvador (Universitat Politècnica de València, Spain)
Nikola Ljubešić (University of Zagreb, Croatia)
Tanja Samardžić (University of Zurich, Switzerland)

Table of Contents

Overview of the DSL Shared Task 2015
Marcos Zampieri, Liling Tan, Nikola Ljubešić, Jörg Tiedemann and Preslav Nakov 1

****INVITED TALK***: Handling and Mining Linguistic Variation in UGC*
Leon Derczynski 10

Distributed Representations of Words and Documents for Discriminating Similar Languages
Marc Franco-Salvador, Paolo Rosso and Francisco Rangel 11

Joint Bayesian Morphology Learning for Dravidian Languages
Arun Kumar, Lluís Padró and Antoni Oliver 17

Use of Transformation-Based Learning in Annotation Pipeline of Igbo, an African Language
Ikechukwu Onyenwe, Mark Hepple, Chinedu Uchechukwu and Ignatius Ezeani 24

****INVITED TALK*** WikiTrans: Swedish-Danish Machine Translation in a Constraint Grammar Framework*
Eckhard Bick 34

Language Identification using Classifier Ensembles
Shervin Malmasi and Mark Dras 35

Discriminating Similar Languages with Token-Based Backoff
Tommi Jauhiainen, Heidi Jauhiainen and Krister Lindén 44

NLEL UPV Autoritas Participation at Discrimination between Similar Languages (DSL) 2015 Shared Task
Raül Fabra Boluda, Francisco Rangel and Paolo Rosso 52

Discriminating between Similar Languages Using PPM
Victoria Bobicev 59

Comparing Approaches to the Identification of Similar Languages
Marcos Zampieri, Binyam Gebrekidan Gebre, Hernani Costa and Josef van Genabith 66

A Two-level Classifier for Discriminating Similar Languages
Judit Ács, László Grad-Gyenge and Thiago Bruno Rodrigues de Rezende Oliveira 73

Experiments in Discriminating Similar Languages
Cyril Goutte and Serge Leger 78

Building Monolingual Word Alignment Corpus for the Greater China Region
fan xu, Xiongfei Xu, Mingwen Wang and Maoxi Li 85

Workshop Program

Thursday, September 10, 2015

Session 1 (chair: Marcos Zampieri)

9:00–9:30 ***Welcome and Overview of the DSL Shared Task***

Overview of the DSL Shared Task 2015
Marcos Zampieri, Liling Tan, Nikola Ljubešić, Jörg Tiedemann and Preslav Nakov

9:30–10:30 ****INVITED TALK***: Handling and Mining Linguistic Variation in UGC*
Leon Derczynski

10:30–11:00 *Distributed Representations of Words and Documents for Discriminating Similar Languages*
Marc Franco-Salvador, Paolo Rosso and Francisco Rangel

11:00–11:30 ***Coffee Break***

Session 2 (chair: Petya Osenova)

11:30–12:00 *Joint Bayesian Morphology Learning for Dravidian Languages*
Arun Kumar, Lluís Padró and Antoni Oliver

12:00–12:30 *Use of Transformation-Based Learning in Annotation Pipeline of Igbo, an African Language*
Ikechukwu Onyenwe, Mark Hepple, Chinedu Uchechukwu and Ignatius Ezeani

12:30–14:00 ***Lunch Break***

Thursday, September 10, 2015 (continued)

Session 3 (chair: Nikola Ljubešić)

14:00-15:00 ****INVITED TALK*** WikiTrans: Swedish-Danish Machine Translation in a Constraint Grammar Framework*
Eckhard Bick

15:00–16:00 Poster Session

Language Identification using Classifier Ensembles
Shervin Malmasi and Mark Dras

Discriminating Similar Languages with Token-Based Backoff
Tommi Jauhiainen, Heidi Jauhiainen and Krister Lindén

NLEL UPV Autoritas Participation at Discrimination between Similar Languages (DSL) 2015 Shared Task
Raül Fabra Boluda, Francisco Rangel and Paolo Rosso

Discriminating between Similar Languages Using PPM
Victoria Bobicev

Comparing Approaches to the Identification of Similar Languages
Marcos Zampieri, Binyam Gebrekidan Gebre, Hernani Costa and Josef van Genabith

A Two-level Classifier for Discriminating Similar Languages
Judit Ács, László Grad-Gyenge and Thiago Bruno Rodrigues de Rezende Oliveira

Experiments in Discriminating Similar Languages
Cyril Goutte and Serge Leger

16:00–16:30 ***Coffee Break***

Thursday, September 10, 2015 (continued)

Session 4 (chair: Nikola Ljubešić)

16:30–17:00 *Building Monolingual Word Alignment Corpus for the Greater China Region*
fan xu, Xiongfei Xu, Mingwen Wang and Maoxi Li

17:00–18:00 Panel Discussion: Marcos Zampieri (moderator), Cyril Goutte, Marc Franco-Salvador, Nikola Ljubešić, and Tanja Samardžić (panelists)

Overview of the DSL Shared Task 2015

Marcos Zampieri[1,2], Liling Tan[1], Nikola Ljubešić[3], Jörg Tiedemann[4], Preslav Nakov[5]
Saarland University, Germany[1]
German Research Center for Artificial Intelligence (DFKI), Germany[2]
University of Zagreb, Croatia[3]
University of Helsinki, Finland[4]
Qatar Computing Research Institute, HBKU, Qatar[5]
marcos.zampieri@uni-saarland.de, liling.tan@uni-saarland.de
jorg.tiedemann@lingfil.uu.se, nljubesi@ffzg.hr, pnakov@qf.org.qa

Abstract

We present the results of the 2nd edition of the Discriminating between Similar Languages (DSL) shared task, which was organized as part of the LT4VarDial'2015 workshop and focused on the identification of very similar languages and language varieties. Unlike in the 2014 edition, in 2015 we had an *Others* category with languages that were not seen on training. Moreover, we had two test datasets: one using the original texts (test set A), and one with named entities replaced by placeholders (test set B). Ten teams participated in the task, and the best-performing system achieved 95.54% average accuracy on test set A, and 94.01% on test set B.

1 Introduction

Identifying the language of an input text is an important step for many natural language processing (NLP) applications, especially when processing speech or social media messages. State-of-the-art language identification systems perform very well when discriminating between unrelated languages on standard datasets. For example, Simões et al. (2014) used TED talks and reported 97% accuracy for discriminating between 25 languages. Yet, this is not a solved problem, and there are a number of scenarios in which language identification has proven to be a very challenging task, especially in the case of very closely-related languages. For example, despite their good overall results, Simões et al. (2014) had really hard time discriminating between Brazilian and European Portuguese, which has made them propose to "remove the Brazilian Portuguese and/or merge it with the European Portuguese variant" to increase system's performance.

So far, researchers in language identification have focused on the following challenges:

- **Increasing the coverage** of language identification systems by extending the number of languages that are recognizable, e.g., Xia et al. (2010) trained a system to identify over 1,000 languages, whereas Brown (2014) developed a language identification tool able to discriminate between over 1,300 languages.

- **Improving the robustness** of language identification systems, e.g., by training on multiple domains and various text types (Lui and Baldwin, 2011).

- **Handling non-standard texts**, e.g., very short (Zubiaga et al., 2014) or involving code-switching (Solorio et al., 2014).

- **Discriminating between very similar languages** (Tiedemann and Ljubešić, 2012), language varieties (Zampieri et al., 2014), and dialects (Sadat et al., 2014; Malmasi et al., 2015).

It has been argued that the latter challenge is one of the main bottlenecks for state-of-the-art language identification systems (Tiedemann and Ljubešić, 2012). Thus, this was the task that we focused on in our shared task on Discriminating between Similar Languages (DSL), which we organized as part of the LT4VarDial'2015 workshop at RANLP'2015.

This is the second edition of the task. The attention received from the research community and the feedback provided by the participants of the first edition motivated us to organize this second DSL shared task, where we made two important changes compared to the first edition.

Proceedings of the Joint Workshop on Language Technology for Closely Related Languages, Varieties and Dialects, pages 1–9,
Hissar, Bulgaria, September 10, 2015.

First, in order to simulate a real-world language identification scenario, we included in the testing dataset some languages that were not present in the training dataset. Moreover, we included a second test set, where we substituted the named entities with placeholders to make the task more challenging and less dependent on the text topic and domain.

The remainder of this paper is organized as follows: Section 2 discusses related work, Section 3 describes the general setup of the task, Section 4 presents the results of the competition, Section 5 summarizes the approaches used by the participants, and Section 6 offers conclusions.

2 Related Work

Language identification has attracted a lot of research attention in recent years, covering a number of similar languages and language varieties such as Malay and Indonesian (Ranaivo-Malançon, 2006), Persian and Dari (Malmasi and Dras, 2015a), Brazilian and European Portuguese (Zampieri and Gebre, 2012), varieties of Mandarin in China, Taiwan and Singapore (Huang and Lee, 2008), and English varieties (Lui and Cook, 2013), among others. This interest has eventually given rise to special shared tasks, which allowed researchers to compare and benchmark various approaches on common standard datasets. Below we will describe some of these shared tasks, including the first edition of the DSL task.

2.1 Related Shared Tasks

There have been a number of language identification shared tasks in recent years. Some were more general, such as the ALTW language identification shared task (Baldwin and Lui, 2010), while others focused on specific datasets or languages. Yet, the DSL shared task is unique as it is the only one to focus specifically on discriminating between *similar languages and language varieties*, providing a standardized dataset for this purpose.

The most closely-related shared task is the DEFT 2010 shared task (Grouin et al., 2010), which targeted language variety identification. However, it focused on French language varieties only, namely on texts from Canada and France. Moreover, it featured a temporal aspect, asking participants to identify *when* a given text was written. This aspect is not part of our DSL shared task, as we focus on contemporary texts.

Another popular research direction has been on language identification on Twitter, which was driven by interest in geolocation prediction for end-user applications (Ljubešić and Kranjčić, 2015). This interest has given rise to the Tweet-LID shared task (Zubiaga et al., 2014), which asked participants to recognize the language of tweet messages, focusing on English and on languages spoken on the Iberian peninsula such as Basque, Catalan, Spanish, and Portuguese. The Shared Task on Language Identification in Code-Switched Data held in 2014 (Solorio et al., 2014) is another related competition, where the focus was on tweets in which users were mixing two or more languages in the same tweet.

2.2 The First Edition of the DSL Task

For the first edition of the task, we compiled the *DSL Corpus Collection* (Tan et al., 2014), or DSLCC v.1.0, which included excerpts from journalistic texts from sources such as the SETimes Corpus[1] (Tyers and Alperen, 2010), HC Corpora[2] and the Leipzig Corpora Collection (Biemann et al., 2007), written in thirteen languages divided into the following six groups: Group A (Bosnian, Croatian, Serbian), Group B (Indonesian, Malay), Group C (Czech, Slovak), Group D (Brazilian Portuguese, European Portuguese), Group E (Peninsular Spanish, Argentine Spanish), and Group F (American English, British English).

In 2014, eight teams built systems and submitted results to the DSL language identification shared task (eight teams participated in the closed and two teams took part in the open condition), and five participants wrote system description papers. The results are summarized in Table 1, where the best-performing submissions, in terms of testing accuracy, are shown in bold.

Team	Closed	Open
NRC-CNRC	**0.957**	-
RAE	0.947	-
UMich	0.932	0.859
UniMelb-NLP	0.918	**0.880**
QMUL	0.906	-
LIRA	0.766	-
UDE	0.681	-
CLCG	0.453	-

Table 1: DSL 2014 results: accuracy.

[1]Published as part of OPUS (Tiedemann, 2012).
[2]`http://www.corpora.heliohost.org/`

The best accuracy in the closed submission track of the 2014 edition of the DSL shared task was achieved by the NRC-CNRC (Goutte et al., 2014) team, which used a two-step classification approach: they first made a prediction about the language group the target text might belong to, and then they selected a language from that language group. Members of this team participated again in 2015 under the name NRC.

The RAE team (Porta and Sancho, 2014) used 'white lists' of words that are used exclusively in a particular language or language variety.

The QMUL team (Purver, 2014) used a linear support vector machines (SVM) classifier with words and characters as features. They further paid special attention to the influence of the cost parameter c on the classifier's performance; this SVM parameter is responsible for the trade-off between maximum margin and classification errors at training time.

Two other participating teams, UMich (King et al., 2014) and UniMelb-NLP (Lui et al., 2014), used Information Gain as a selection criterion (Yang and Pedersen, 1997) to select a subset of features, trying to improve classification accuracy. The UniMelb-NLP team experimented with different classifiers and features, and eventually obtained their best results using their own software, *langid.py* (Lui and Baldwin, 2012).

The UMich and UniMelb-NLP teams compiled and used additional training resources and were the only teams to submit open submissions. However, the performance of these open submissions were worse than what they achieved in their closed submissions: accuracy dropped from 93.2% to 85.9% for UMich, and from 91.8% to 88.0% for UniMelb-NLP.

This worse performance of the open submissions was quite surprising. We had a closer look, and we hypothesized that this could be due to the abundance of named entities in our datasets. For example, participating systems could learn that a text that talks about Brazilian places, companies, politicians, etc. is likely to be in Brazilian Portuguese. These are legitimate features, but they are about the topic of the text and do not reflect linguistic characteristics, which we were hoping participants would focus on. Thus, in the 2015 edition of the task, we created two test sets, one containing the original texts, and one where we substituted the named entities with placeholders.

3 Task Setup

In this section, we describe the general setup of the DSL 2015 shared and unshared task tracks, the changes in v2.0 of the DSLCC dataset compared to v1.0, and the task schedule.

3.1 The Shared Task Track

The setup of the 2015 DSL *Shared Task* is similar to the one for the 2014 edition. However, we created a new updated v2.0 of DSLCC (Tan et al., 2014), extending it with new languages. We provided participants with standard splits into training and development subsets, and we further prepared two test sets, as described in Section 3.3 below. As in 2014, teams could make two types of submissions (for each team, we allowed up to three runs per submission type; in the official ranking, we included the run with the highest score only):

- **Closed submission:** Using only the DSLCC v2.0 for training.

- **Open submission:** Using any dataset other than DSLCC v2.0 for training.[3]

3.2 The Unshared Task Track

Along with the Shared Task, this year we proposed an *Unshared Task* track inspired by the unshared task in PoliInformatics held in 2014 (Smith et al., 2014). For this track, teams were allowed to use any version of DSLCC to investigate differences between similar languages and language varieties using NLP methods. We were interested in studying questions like these:

- Are there fundamental grammatical differences in a language group?

- What are the most distinctive lexical choices for each language?

- Which text representation is most suitable to investigate language variation?

- What is the impact of lexical and grammatical variation on NLP applications?

Although eleven teams subscribed for the Unshared Task track, none of them ended up submiting a paper for it. Therefore, below we will only discuss the Shared Task track.

Language/Variety	ISO Code
Bosnian	*bs*
Croatian	*hr*
Serbian	*sr*
Indonesian	*id*
Malay	*my*
Czech	*cz*
Slovak	*sk*
Brazilian Portuguese	*pt-BR*
European Portuguese	*pt-PT*
Argentine Spanish	*es-AR*
Castilian Spanish	*es-ES*
Bulgarian	*bg*
Macedonian	*mk*
Others	*xx*

Table 2: DSLCC v2.0: the languages included in the corpus grouped by similarity. *Others* is a mixture of Catalan, Russian, Slovene, and Tagalog.

3.3 The DSLCC v2.0 Dataset

Version 2.0 of DSLCC (Tan et al., 2014) contains a total of 308,000 examples divided into fourteen language classes with 22,000 examples per class. Each example is a short text excerpt of 20–100 tokens,[4] sampled from journalistic texts colected from the same sources as in DSLCC v1.0. The fourteen classes are shown in Table 2; they represent thirteen languages and language varieties and one mixed class with documents written in four other languages, namely: Catalan, Russian, Slovene, and Tagalog.[5] We included the mixed Others class in order to emulate a real-world language identification scenario in which 'unknown' but similar languages might appear, thus making the task more challenging.

We partitioned the 22,000 examples for each language class into three parts as follows: 18,000 examples for training, 2,000 for development, and 2,000 for testing. We then further subdivided each test set into two test sets, A and B, each containing 1,000 instances per language. We kept the texts in test set A unchanged, but we preprocessed those in test set B by replacing all named entities with placeholders.[6]

We substituted the named entities with placeholders in order to avoid topic bias in classification and to evaluate the extent to which proper names can influence classifiers' performance.

As an example, here we show a Portuguese and a Spanish text: first the original texts, then versions thereof with named entities substituted by placeholders *#NE#*.

(1) Rui Nobre dos Santos explica que "a empresa pretende começar a exportar para Angola e Moçambique, em 2010", objectivo que está traçado desde 2007 "mas que ainda não foi possível concretizar", e aumentar as exportações para o Brasil.

(2) El jueves pasado se conoció que Schoklender había renunciado a su cargo, según la prensa local por una pelea con su hermano, que también trabaja en la entidad, al parecer por desacuerdos en el manejo de los fondos para la construcción de viviendas populares.

(3) Compara #NE# este sistema às indulgências vendidas pelo #NE# na #NE# #NE# quando os fiéis compravam a redenção das suas almas dando dinheiro aos padres.

(4) La cinta, que hoy se estrena en nuestro país, competirá contra #NE# la #NE#, de #NE#, #NE#, de #NE#, #NE#, de #NE# á, #NE# above all, de #NE#, y con la ganadora del #NE# de #NE#, #NE# A #NE# #NE#, de #NE#.

3.4 Shared Task Schedule

The second DSL shared task was open for two months, spanning from May 20, 2015, when the training data was released, to July 20, 2015, when the paper submissions were due. Teams had just over a month to train their systems before the release of the test data. The schedule of the DSL shared task 2015 is shown in Table 3.

Event	Date
Training set released	May 20, 2015
Test set released	June 22, 2015
Submissions due	June 24, 2015
Results announced	June 26, 2015
Paper submissions due	July 20, 2015

Table 3: The DSL 2015 Shared Task schedule.

[3]Training on DSLCC v1.0 also makes a submission open.

[4]In DSLCC v1.0, texts could be longer than 100 tokens.

[5]For the Unshared Task track, we further made available DSLCC v2.1, which extended DSLCC v2.0 with Mexican Spanish and Macanese Portuguese data.

[6]The script we used to substitute named entities with placeholders is available here: `https://github.com/Simdiva/DSL-Task/blob/master/blindNE.py`

Team	Closed (Normal)	Closed (No NEs)	Open (Normal)	Open (No NEs)	System Description Paper
BOICEV	✓	✓	-	-	(Bobicev, 2015)
BRUNIBP	✓	-	-	-	(Ács et al., 2015)
INRIA	✓	-	-	-	-
MAC	✓	✓	-	-	(Malmasi and Dras, 2015b)
MMS*	✓	✓	-	-	(Zampieri et al., 2015)
NLEL	✓	✓	✓	✓	(Fabra-Boluda et al., 2015)
NRC	✓	✓	✓	✓	(Goutte and Léger, 2015)
OSEVAL	-	-	✓	✓	-
PRHLT	✓	✓	-	-	(Franco-Salvador et al., 2015)
SUKI	✓	✓	-	-	(Jauhiainen et al., 2015a)
Total	**9**	**7**	**3**	**3**	**8**

Table 4: The participating teams in the DSL 2015 Shared Task.

4 Results

In this section, we present the results of the 2nd edition of the DSL shared task.[7] Most of the participating teams used DSLCC v2.0 only, and thus took part in the closed submission track. Yet, three of the teams collected additional data or used DSLCC v1.0, and thereby participated in the open submission.

4.1 Submitted Runs

A total of 24 teams subscribed to participate in the shared task, 10 of them submitted official runs, and 8 of the latter also wrote system description papers. These numbers represent a slight increase in participation compared to the 2014 edition, which attracted 22 teams, 8 submissions, and 5 system description papers.

Table 4 gives information about the ten teams that submitted runs, indicating the tracks they participated in. The table also includes references to their system description papers, when applicable. As one of the members of the MMS team was a shared task organizer, we have decided to mark the team with a star; and we do so in all tables. Still, this team did not have any unfair advantage, and competed under the same conditions as the rest.

4.2 Closed Submission

As in 2014, most teams chose to participate in the closed submission: 9 out of 10. All these 9 teams submitted runs for test set A, and their results are shown in Table 5. We can see that the best result was 95.54% accuracy, achieved by the MAC team, followed very closely by MMS and NRC, which both achieved 95.24% accuracy.

Rank	Team	Accuracy
1	MAC	95.54
2-3	MMS*	95.24
2-3	NRC	95.24
4	SUKI	94.67
5	BOBICEV	94.14
6	BRUNIBP	93.66
7	PRHLT	92.74
8	INRIA	83.91
9	NLEL	64.04

Table 5: Closed submission results for test set A.

Seven of the nine teams who took part in the open submission submitted runs for test set B; the results are shown in Table 6. We can see a drop in accuracy, which is to be expected. Once again, the MAC team performed best with 94.01% accuracy, followed by SUKI and NRC with 93.02% and 93.01%, respectively.

Rank	Team	Accuracy
1	MAC	94.01
2	SUKI	93.02
3	NRC	93.01
4	MMS*	92.78
5	BOBICEV	92.22
6	PRHLT	90.80
7	NLEL	62.78

Table 6: Closed submission results for test set B.

4.3 Open Submission

Three teams participated in the open submission track: NRC, NLEL, and OSEVAL. Their results are shown in Table 7. Unlike DSL 2014 (see Table 1), two of these teams, NRC and NLEL, managed to achieve better accuracy in the open submission than in the closed one on test set A.[8]

[7]More detailed evaluation results can be found at `https://github.com/Simdiva/DSL-Task/blob/master/DSL2015-results.md`

[8]OSEVAL did not participate in the closed submission.

Rank	Team	Accuracy
1	NRC	95.65
2	NLEL	91.84
3	OSEVAL	76.17

Table 7: Open submission results for test set A.

This could be related to the availability of DSLCC v1.0 as an obvious additional resource. The NRC system description paper indeed confirms that they used DSLCC v1.0 (Goutte and Léger, 2015), and points out that this yielded 10% error reduction and 0.4% absolute boost in accuracy. In contrast, teams that submitted open submissions to the 2014 edition did not have access to such a well-matching additional resource.

The open submission results for test set B are shown in Table 8: we can see once again improved performance for NLEL and NRC.[9]

Rank	Team	Accuracy
1	NRC	93.41
2	NLEL	89.56
3	OSEVAL	75.30

Table 8: Open submission results for test set B.

4.4 Results per Language

Not all language pairs and groups of languages are equally difficult to distinguish from the rest. We wanted to have a closer look at this, and thus we plotted for each language the mean accuracy across all submissions and the interquartal range, excluding outliers: accuracy results for test sets A and B in the closed submission track are shown in Figures 1 and 2, respectively.

We can see that, on test set A, systems performed very well when discriminating between the languages in the following pairs: Bulgarian–Macedonian, Czech–Slovak, and Indonesian–Malay. On test set B, distinguishing between Indonesian and Malay was difficult, maybe because there were many country-specific named entities in Indonesian and Malay texts, which were helping to discriminate between them on test set A. Overall, the most challenging groups are Bosnian–Croatian–Serbian, as well as the Spanish and the Portuguese varieties, which corroborates the findings of the first edition of the DSL shared task.

[9] Note, however, that NLEL reported having a bug, which is an alternative explanation for the low performance of their closed submission runs.

5 Approaches

The participants used a variety of classifiers and features, which, in our opinion, confirms the DSL shared task as a very fruitful scientific endeavor for both organizers and participants.

The best system in the closed submission was that of the MAC team (Malmasi and Dras, 2015b). They used an ensemble of SVM classifiers, and features such as character n-grams (n=1,2,...,6) and word unigrams and bigrams.

The NRC team (Goutte and Léger, 2015) included members of the NRC-CNRC team, which won the DSL closed submission track in 2014. Both in 2014 and now, they used two-stage classification, which first predicts the language group, and then chooses between languages or varieties within this group. The team achieved very strong results this year, ranking second in the closed submission on test set A, third on test set B, and first in the open submission on both test sets A and B. Two other participants used two-stage classification: NLEL (Fabra-Boluda et al., 2015) and BRUniBP (Ács et al., 2015).

The MMS team experimented with three approaches (Zampieri et al., 2015), and their best run combined TF.IDF weighting and an SVM classifier, which was previously successfully applied to native language identification (Gebre et al., 2013).

The SUKI team (Jauhiainen et al., 2015a) used *token-based backoff*, which was previously applied to general-purpose language identification (Jauhiainen et al., 2015b).

The BOBICEV team applied *prediction by partial matching*, which had not been used for this task before (Bobicev, 2015).

Finally, the PRHLT team (Franco-Salvador et al., 2015) used word and sentence vectors, which is to our knowledge the first attempt to apply them to discriminating between similar languages.

6 Conclusion

The second edition of the DSL shared task, with its focus on similar languages, continues to fill an important gap in language identification research. It allows researchers to experiment with different algorithms and methods and to evaluate their systems for discriminating between related languages and language varieties. Compared to the first edition, this year we observed an increase in team participation, which shows the continuous interest of the research community in this task.

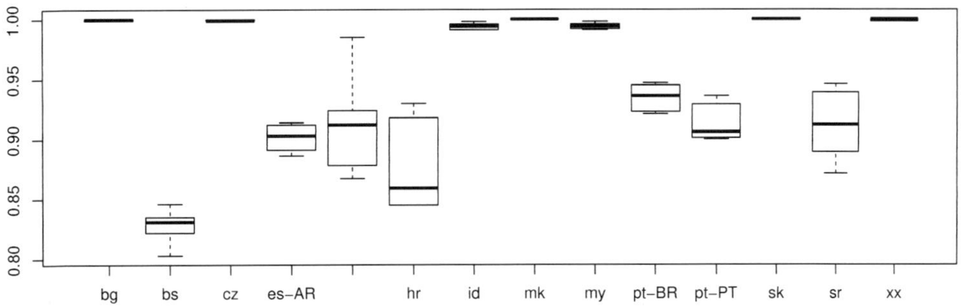

Figure 1: Accuracy per language: closed submission, test set A.

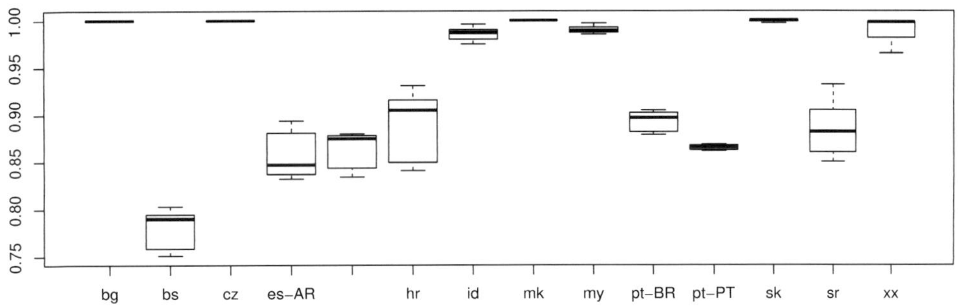

Figure 2: Accuracy per language: closed submission, test set B.

In total, 24 teams registered to participate, and 10 made submissions. The best-performing system in the closed submission track was that of MAC (Malmasi and Dras, 2015b), and it achieved 95.54% accuracy on test set A and 94.01% on test set B, using an ensemble of SVM classifiers. The winner in the open submission track NRC (Goutte and Léger, 2015) achieved 95.65% accuracy on test set A, and 93.41% on test set B, using two-stage classification.

Unlike the 2014 edition, in 2015 we had the *Others* category with languages not seen on training. Moreover, we had a second test set, where named entities were replaced by placeholders.

Comparing the results for the two test sets, (*i*) the original vs. (*ii*) the one with placeholders, has shown that the accuracy on the latter dropped by about 2% absolute for all teams. However, the impact of substituting named entities was not as great as we had imagined, especially for language groups for which the accuracy was already close or equal to 100% (except for Indonesian–Malay). This suggests that closely-related languages and language varieties have distinctive properties that classifiers are able to recognize and learn.

For a possible third edition of the DSL Shared Task, we would like to explore the possibility to include dialects in the dataset. The case of Arabic is particularly interesting, and has already attracted research attention (Sadat et al., 2014). Unfortunately, Arabic dialects do not have official status and thus are not common in journalistic texts; thus, we would need to compile a heterogeneous dataset including other genres as well.

Another interesting aspect, which we did not study explictly in the first two editions of the DSL Shared Task (even though the instances in v1.0 and v2.0 of DSLCC did have different length distributions), but which we would like to explore in the future, is the influence of text length on the classification performance. See (Malmasi et al., 2015) for a relevant discussion.

Acknowledgements

We would like to thank all participants in the DSL Shared Task for their valuable suggestions and comments. We further thank the LT4VarDial Program Committee for thoroughly reviewing the system papers and the shared task report.

References

Judit Ács, László Grad-Gyenge, and Thiago Bruno Rodrigues de Rezende Oliveira. 2015. A two-level classifier for discriminating similar languages. In *Proceedings of the Joint Workshop on Language Technology for Closely Related Languages, Varieties and Dialects*, LT4VarDial '15, pages 73–77, Hissar, Bulgaria.

Timothy Baldwin and Marco Lui. 2010. Multilingual language identification: ALTW 2010 shared task data. In *Proceedings of Australasian Language Technology Association Workshop*, ALTA '10, pages 4–7, Melbourne, Australia.

Chris Biemann, Gerhard Heyer, Uwe Quasthoff, and Matthias Richter. 2007. The Leipzig corpora collection-monolingual corpora of standard size. In *Proceedings of Corpus Linguistics*, Birmingham, UK.

Victoria Bobicev. 2015. Discriminating between similar languages using PPM. In *Proceedings of the Joint Workshop on Language Technology for Closely Related Languages, Varieties and Dialects*, LT4VarDial '15, pages 59–65, Hissar, Bulgaria.

Ralf Brown. 2014. Non-linear mapping for improved identification of 1300+ languages. In *Proceedings of the 2014 Conference on Empirical Methods in Natural Language Processing*, EMNLP '14, pages 627–632, Doha, Qatar.

Raül Fabra-Boluda, Francisco Rangel, and Paolo Rosso. 2015. NLEL UPV autoritas participation at Discrimination between Similar Languages (DSL) 2015 shared task. In *Proceedings of the Joint Workshop on Language Technology for Closely Related Languages, Varieties and Dialects*, LT4VarDial '15, pages 52–58, Hissar, Bulgaria.

Marc Franco-Salvador, Paolo Rosso, and Francisco Rangel. 2015. Distributed representations of words and documents for discriminating similar languages. In *Proceedings of the Joint Workshop on Language Technology for Closely Related Languages, Varieties and Dialects*, LT4VarDial '15, pages 11–16, Hissar, Bulgaria.

Binyam Gebrekidan Gebre, Marcos Zampieri, Peter Wittenburg, and Tom Heskes. 2013. Improving native language identification with TF-IDF weighting. In *Proceedings of the Eighth Workshop on Innovative Use of NLP for Building Educational Applications*, BEA8, pages 216–223, Atlanta, GA, USA.

Cyril Goutte and Serge Léger. 2015. Experiments in discriminating similar languages. In *Proceedings of the Joint Workshop on Language Technology for Closely Related Languages, Varieties and Dialects*, LT4VarDial '15, pages 78–84, Hissar, Bulgaria.

Cyril Goutte, Serge Léger, and Marine Carpuat. 2014. The NRC system for discriminating similar languages. In *Proc. of the Workshop on Applying NLP Tools to Similar Languages, Varieties and Dialects*, VarDial '14, pages 139–145, Dublin, Ireland.

Cyril Grouin, Dominic Forest, Lyne Da Sylva, Patrick Paroubek, and Pierre Zweigenbaum. 2010. Présentation et résultats du défi fouille de texte DEFT2010 où et quand un article de presse a-t-il été écrit? In *Actes du sixième Défi Fouille de Textes*, DEFT '10, Montreal, Canada.

Chu-ren Huang and Lung-hao Lee. 2008. Contrastive approach towards text source classification based on top-bag-of-word similarity. In *Proceedings of 22nd Pacific Asia Conference on Language, Information and Computation*, PACLIC '08, pages 404–410, Cebu City, Philippines.

Tommi Jauhiainen, Heidi Jauhiainen, and Krister Lindén. 2015a. Discriminating similar languages with token-based backoff. In *Proceedings of the Joint Workshop on Language Technology for Closely Related Languages, Varieties and Dialects*, LT4VarDial '15, pages 44–51, Hissar, Bulgaria.

Tommi Jauhiainen, Krister Lindén, and Heidi Jauhiainen. 2015b. Language set identification in noisy synthetic multilingual documents. In *Proceedings of the 16th International Conference on Computational Linguistics and Intelligent Text Processing*, CICLING '15, pages 633–643, Cairo, Egypt.

Ben King, Dragomir Radev, and Steven Abney. 2014. Experiments in sentence language identification with groups of similar languages. In *Proceedings of the 1st Workshop on Applying NLP Tools to Similar Languages, Varieties and Dialects*, VarDial '14, pages 146–154, Dublin, Ireland.

Nikola Ljubešić and Denis Kranjčić. 2015. Discriminating between closely related languages on Twitter. *Informatica*, 39(1).

Marco Lui and Timothy Baldwin. 2011. Cross-domain feature selection for language identification. In *Proceedings of 5th International Joint Conference on Natural Language Processing*, IJCNLP '11, pages 553–561, Chiang Mai, Thailand.

Marco Lui and Timothy Baldwin. 2012. Langid.py: An off-the-shelf language identification tool. In *Proceedings of the ACL 2012 System Demonstrations*, ACL '12, pages 25–30, Jeju Island, Korea.

Marco Lui and Paul Cook. 2013. Classifying English documents by national dialect. In *Proceedings of Australasian Language Technology Workshop*, ALTA '13, pages 5–15, Brisbane, Australia.

Marco Lui, Ned Letcher, Oliver Adams, Long Duong, Paul Cook, and Timothy Baldwin. 2014. Exploring methods and resources for discriminating similar languages. In *Proceedings of the 1st Workshop on Applying NLP Tools to Similar Languages, Varieties and Dialects*, VarDial '14, pages 129–138, Dublin, Ireland.

Shervin Malmasi and Mark Dras. 2015a. Automatic language identification for Persian and Dari texts. In *Proceedings of the 14th Conference of the Pacific Association for Computational Linguistics*, PACLING '15, pages 59–64, Bali, Indonesia.

Shervin Malmasi and Mark Dras. 2015b. Language identification using classifier ensembles. In *Proceedings of the Joint Workshop on Language Technology for Closely Related Languages, Varieties and Dialects*, LT4VarDial '15, pages 35–43, Hissar, Bulgaria.

Shervin Malmasi, Eshrag Refaee, and Mark Dras. 2015. Arabic dialect identification using a parallel multidialectal corpus. In *Proceedings of the 14th Conference of the Pacific Association for Computational Linguistics*, PACLING '15, pages 209–217, Bali, Indonesia.

Jordi Porta and José-Luis Sancho. 2014. Using maximum entropy models to discriminate between similar languages and varieties. In *Proceedings of the 1st Workshop on Applying NLP Tools to Similar Languages, Varieties and Dialects*, VarDial '14, pages 120–128, Dublin, Ireland.

Matthew Purver. 2014. A simple baseline for discriminating similar language. In *Proceedings of the 1st Workshop on Applying NLP Tools to Similar Languages, Varieties and Dialect*, VarDial '14, pages 155–160, Dublin, Ireland.

Bali Ranaivo-Malançon. 2006. Automatic identification of close languages - case study: Malay and Indonesian. *ECTI Transactions on Computer and Information Technology*, 2:126–134.

Fatiha Sadat, Farnazeh Kazemi, and Atefeh Farzindar. 2014. Automatic identification of Arabic language varieties and dialects in social media. In *Proceedings of the Second Workshop on Natural Language Processing for Social Media*, SocialNLP '14, pages 22–27, Dublin, Ireland.

Alberto Simões, José João Almeida, and Simon D Byers. 2014. Language identification: a neural network approach. In *Proceedings of the 3rd Symposium on Languages, Applications and Technologies*, SLATE '14, pages 252–265, Dagstuhl, Germany.

Noah A. Smith, Claire Cardie, Anne L. Washington, and John D. Wilkerson. 2014. Overview of the 2014 NLP unshared task in PoliInformatics. In *Proceedings of the Workshop on Language Technologies and Computational Social Science*, pages 5–7, Baltimore, Maryland, USA.

Thamar Solorio, Elizabeth Blair, Suraj Maharjan, Steven Bethard, Mona Diab, Mahmoud Ghoneim, Abdelati Hawwari, Fahad AlGhamdi, Julia Hirschberg, Alison Chang, and Pascale Fung. 2014. Overview for the first shared task on language identification in code-switched data. In *Proceedings of the First Workshop on Computational Approaches to Code Switching*, pages 62–72, Doha, Qatar.

Liling Tan, Marcos Zampieri, Nikola Ljubešić, and Jörg Tiedemann. 2014. Merging comparable data sources for the discrimination of similar languages: The DSL corpus collection. In *Proceedings of The Workshop on Building and Using Comparable Corpora*, BUCC '14, pages 6–10, Reykjavik, Iceland.

Jörg Tiedemann and Nikola Ljubešić. 2012. Efficient discrimination between closely related languages. In *Proceedings of the 24th International Conference on Computational Linguistics*, COLING '12, pages 2619–2634, Mumbai, India.

Jörg Tiedemann. 2012. Parallel data, tools and interfaces in OPUS. In *Proceedings of the International Conference on Language Resources and Evaluation*, LREC '12, pages 2214–2218, Istanbul, Turkey.

Francis Tyers and Murat Serdar Alperen. 2010. South-East European Times: A parallel corpus of Balkan languages. In *Proceedings of the LREC workshop on Exploitation of multilingual resources and tools for Central and (South) Eastern European Languages*, Valetta, Malta.

Fei Xia, Carrie Lewis, and William D Lewis. 2010. The problems of language identification within hugely multilingual data sets. In *Proceedings of the Seventh International Conference on Language Resources and Evaluation*, LREC '10, pages 2790–2797, Valetta, Malta.

Yiming Yang and Jan O. Pedersen. 1997. A comparative study on feature selection in text categorization. In *Proceedings of the Fourteenth International Conference on Machine Learning*, ICML '97, pages 412–420, Nashville, Tennessee, USA.

Marcos Zampieri and Binyam Gebrekidan Gebre. 2012. Automatic identification of language varieties: The case of Portuguese. In *Proceedings of KONVENS*, pages 233–237, Vienna, Austria.

Marcos Zampieri, Liling Tan, Nikola Ljubešić, and Jörg Tiedemann. 2014. A report on the DSL shared task 2014. In *Proceedings of the Workshop on Applying NLP Tools to Similar Languages, Varieties and Dialects*, VarDial '14, pages 58–67, Dublin, Ireland.

Marcos Zampieri, Binyam Gebrekidan Gebre, Hernani Costa, and Josef van Genabith. 2015. Comparing approaches to the identification of similar languages. In *Proceedings of the Joint Workshop on Language Technology for Closely Related Languages, Varieties and Dialects*, LT4VarDial '15, pages 66–72, Hissar, Bulgaria.

Arkaitz Zubiaga, Inaki San Vicente, Pablo Gamallo, José Ramom Pichel, Inaki Alegria, Nora Aranberri, Aitzol Ezeiza, and Vıctor Fresno. 2014. Overview of tweetLID: Tweet language identification at SEPLN 2014. In *Proceedings of the Tweet Language Identification Workshop*, TweetLID '14, pages 1–11, Girona, Spain.

Handling and Mining Linguistic Variation in UGC (invited talk)

Leon Derczynski
Department of Computer Science
The University of Sheffield
leon@dcs.shef.ac.uk

1 Abstract

Across its many forms, user-generated content (UGC) acts as a sample of all human discourse. It has been harder to process this type of text with traditional tools. People have even looked at normalising this text to look like the data that traditional tools are used to. This talk examines the kind of variation we see in user-generated content, and contrary to the trend of normalisation, not only presents methods for coping with the noise without changing it, but also goes on to explain the many kinds of latent information expressed by the stable, consistent linguistic variation seen across society and the internet.

2 Biography

Dr. Leon Derczynski is a Research Associate in the University of Sheffield's NLP group. He has worked on the forefront of social media language processing since 2012, developing and releasing tools to the community and in GATE, and is applying this by current work on multiple EU projects centred around detecting and predicting rumours and false claims on the web.

Proceedings of the Joint Workshop on Language Technology for Closely Related Languages, Varieties and Dialects, page 10,
Hissar, Bulgaria, September 10, 2015.

Distributed Representations of Words and Documents for Discriminating Similar Languages

Marc Franco-Salvador[1], **Paolo Rosso**[1], and **Francisco Rangel**[1,2]
[1] Universitat Politècnica de València, Spain
[2] Autoritas Consulting, S.A., Spain
mfranco@prhlt.upv.es, prosso@dsic.upv.es,
francisco.rangel@autoritas.es

Abstract

Discriminating between similar languages or language varieties aims to detect lexical and semantic variations in order to classify these varieties of languages. In this work we describe the system built by the Pattern Recognition and Human Language Technology (PRHLT) research center - Universitat Politècnica de València and Autoritas Consulting for the Discriminating between similar languages (DSL) 2015 shared task. In order to determine the language group of similar languages, we first employ a simple approach based on distances with language prototypes with 99.8% accuracy in the test sets. For classifying intra-group languages we focus on the use of distributed representations of words and documents using the continuous Skip-gram model. Experimental results of classification of languages in 14 categories yielded accuracies of 92.7% and 90.8% when classifying unmodified texts and text with hidden named entities, respectively.

1 Introduction

Automatic language identification is considered a solved problem in a regular scenario. McNamee (2005) demonstrated how even the most simple of the methods, based on language prototypes of term frequencies, is able to achieve almost 100% accuracy of classification. However, it is far to be solved if we consider the classification of short text, mixed content and when discriminating between language varieties and similar languages. Carter et al. (2013) investigated the language identification of short and noisy text of several European languages using Twitter data, and justified the difficulty of classification in this domain. Gottron and Lipka (2010) studied the identification of European languages in news headlines and single unambiguous words. They demonstrated the impact of the length in the accuracy of classification.

The identification of varieties of the same language has been related to author profiling (Rangel et al., 2013; Rangel et al., 2014; Rangel and Rosso, 2015), which aims to identify the linguistic profile of an author on the basis of his writing style, and to determine author's traits such as gender, age and personality. Variety identification differs from the aforementioned language identification works in terms of difficulty due to the high syntactic and semantic similarities. Accuracy of classification is reduced from 90-100% to values closer to 80%. In (Zampieri and Gebre, 2012) the authors investigated varieties of Portuguese applying different features such as word and character n-grams. Similarly, in (Sadat et al., 2014) the authors differentiate between six different varieties of Arabic in blogs and forums using character n-grams. Concerning Spanish language varieties, in (Maier and Gómez-Rodríguez, 2014) the authors employed meta-learning to classify tweets from Argentina, Chile, Colombia, Mexico and Spain. Zubiaga et al. (2014) overviews the results of the shared task of tweet language identification organized at SEPLN'2014. A more recent work (Franco-Salvador et al., 2015), explored the use of techniques based on embeddings to model semantics and evaluated using the HispaBlogs[1] dataset, a new collection of Spanish blogs from five different countries: Argentina, Chile, Mexico, Peru and Spain. The proposed approach demonstrated to achieve remarkable performance and to be less sensitive to over-fitting than the compared state-of-the-art approaches.

In order to illustrate that language identification is not a solved problem, the Discrimi-

[1]The HispaBlogs dataset can be downloaded at: https://github.com/autoritas/RD-Lab/tree/master/data/HispaBlogs

Proceedings of the Joint Workshop on Language Technology for Closely Related Languages, Varieties and Dialects, pages 11–16,
Hissar, Bulgaria, September 10, 2015. ©2015 Association for Computational Linguistics

nating between similar languages (DSL) shared task (Zampieri et al., 2014; Zampieri et al., 2015) is organized. This task encourages participants to submit systems in order to identify the language of short texts of several groups of similar and varieties of languages (Tan et al., 2014). Goutte et al. (2014) achieved the best results of the 2014 edition with a combination of different kernels using Support Vector Machines (SVM) (Chang and Lin, 2011) and word and character n-gram features. This year, the task aims to identify the language of six groups of texts containing similar and varieties of languages (see Table 1) and a group containing texts written in a set of other languages.

In this work we evaluate the 2015 shared task by adapting the approach presented in (Franco-Salvador et al., 2015). We first use an approach based on distances with language prototypes to determine the language group, and next we classify the language using the continuous Skip-gram model to generate distributed representations of words, i.e., n-dimensional vectors –applying further refinements in order to be able to use them in documents. In addition, we use the Sentence Vector variation to directly generate representations of documents. Motivations behind evaluating this approach in the DSL shared task are: i) analyse the performance when classifying not only varieties of languages but also similar ones; and ii) determine the validity of the approach to work with considerably shorter texts (sentences) compared to the blogs with 10 post per user that were used as single instance in the past.

The rest of the paper is structured as follows. Section 2 presents the approach we adapted for the shared task, Section 3 details our evaluation, and in Section 4 we provide our conclusions and future works. Additional analysis and comparison with the other submitted systems are available in the 2015 shared task overview (Zampieri et al., 2015).

2 Discriminating Similar Languages

In this section we detail the approach we used for discriminating between similar languages. We first describe the pre-processing we employed, next we present the method for classifying sentences among language groups of similar languages (inter-group classifier), and finally we review the distributed vector-based approach for identifying the language within groups of similar languages (intra-group classifier).

2.1 Data Pre-processing

For both inter- and intra-group classifiers, we preprocessed the text with tokenization, removed the tokens of length one, and those including numbers or punctuation. In addition, to ease the learning with the considerably low number of text available for generating the distributed vectors and to reduce ambiguity, we lowercased the input words and performed phrase detection for the intra-group classifier.

2.2 Inter-group Classifier

To classify sentences among groups of similar languages, we used a similar and simplified version of McNamee (2005). Having a training set Tr containing sentences belonging to one of the Lg language groups, we first generated the set of prototypes $proto_{Lg}$ of each language group using a bag-of-words representation. Next, for each input sentence $t = (w_1, w_2, ..., w_n)$ of the test set Te, we compute the language group g as follows:

$$g = \text{argmax}_{pr_g \in proto_{Lg}} \sum_{i}^{n} |w_i \cap pr_g|, \quad (1)$$

where basically we determine the language group of a sentence as the group with the higher number of common words. Note that the sentence is represented as a list and, consequently, we allow for word repetitions, contrary to the prototypes. Using this method with the development partition, we achieved a 99.99% of accuracy in the inter-group classification, and demonstrated again that the task is trivial among considerably different languages.

2.3 Intra-group Classifier

To identify the language of sentences of similar and varieties of languages, we adapted the approach of our previous work (Franco-Salvador et al., 2015). We generated vector representations of sentences in two different ways. In Section 2.3.1 we describe how creating sentence vectors as a combination of distributed word vectors. Next, in Section 2.3.2 we describe an alternative and related approach to directly generate distributed representations of sentences. In Section 2.3.3 we describe the algorithms we chose for classification.

2.3.1 Generating Sentence Vectors from Word Vectors

The use of log-linear models has been proposed (Mikolov et al., 2013a) as an efficient alternative to generate distributed representations, since they reduce the complexity of the hidden layer thereby improving efficiency. In this section we use the continuous Skip-gram model (Mikolov et al., 2013a; Mikolov et al., 2013b) to generate distributed representations (e.g. vectors) of words. It is an iterative algorithm which attempts to maximize the classification of the context surrounding a word. Formally, given a word w_t, and its surrounding words w_{t-c}, $w_{t-c+1}, \ldots, w_{t+c}$ inside a window of size $2c+1$, the training objective is to maximize the average of the log probability:

$$\frac{1}{T}\sum_{t=1}^{T}\sum_{-c\leq j\leq c, j\neq 0}\log p(w_{t+j}|w_t) \qquad (2)$$

Although $p(w_{t+j}|w_t)$ can be estimated using the softmax function (Barto, 1998), its normalization depends on the vocabulary size W which makes its usage impractical for high values of W. For this reason, more computationally efficient alternatives are used instead. In this work we used the negative sampling (Mikolov et al., 2013b), a simplified version of the Noise Contrastive Estimation (NCE) (Gutmann and Hyvärinen, 2012; Mnih and Teh, 2012), which basically uses logistic regression to distinguish the target word from a noise distribution, having k negative samples for each word. Experimental results in Mikolov et al. (2013a) show that the Skip-gram model obtains better results at semantic level than other log-linear alternatives such as the continuous Bag-of-words model, and Mikolov et al. (2013b) offered identical conclusions for the negative sampling compared to NCE and Hierarchical softmax (Morin and Bengio, 2005), hence the election of our models.

In order to combine the word vectors generated with the Skip-gram model, having a list of vectors $(\vec{w}_1, \vec{w}_2, \ldots, \vec{w}_n)$ belonging to the words of a sentence, we generated a vector representation $\vec{v}$ of its content by estimating the average of their dimensions: $\vec{v} = n^{-1}\sum_{i=1}^{n}\vec{w}_i$. We refer to such document vector representation as *Skip-gram* in the evaluation section.

2.3.2 Learning Sentence Vectors

Sentence vectors (SenVec) (Le and Mikolov, 2014) follows Skip-gram architecture to train a special vector $\vec{v}$ representing the complete sentence. Basically, the model uses all the words of the sentence as context to train the vector representing its content. In contrast, the original Skip-gram model employs a fixed size window to determine the context (surrounding words) of the iterated words of a sentence.

2.3.3 Classifying distributed vectors

To classify the distributed vectors of the combination of words, we used a logistic classifier (Skip-gram + LG (run1)). For that model we employed also an SVM classifier (Skip-gram + SVM (run2)) with radial basis function kernel and cost 10. Finally, SenVec vectors were classified using a logistic classifier (SenVec + LG (run3)). At this point, we must point out that the test sentences contain words which are not present in the training set. Obviously, for those words we have not learned a distributed vector but we have the initial random vector we could use to train it. Despite we could directly ignore and remove those words, the experiments with the development partition showed that there is not loss of performance when we include those vectors, and even in some configurations, e.g. Skip-gram + LG, provided a very slight improvement (0.6%). We hypothesize that this insertion of noise in the vectors may help the classifiers to determine the frontiers among languages, and we kept them in our experiments.

3 Evaluation

In this section we evaluate our systems for the DSL 2015 shared task. Given a labelled collection of training sentences Tr belonging to a set of L languages, and a collection of test sentences Te, the task is to classify each sentence $t \in Te$ into one of the languages $l \in L$ using the labelled sentences of Tr.

3.1 Dataset and Methodology

We evaluated our system with the DSL Corpus Collection (Tan et al., 2014) of this edition (DSLCC v. 2.0). This dataset contains sentences in Bulgarian, Macedonian, Serbian, Croatian, Bosnian, Czech, Slovak, Argentinian Spanish, Peninsular Spanish, Brazilian Portuguese, European Portuguese, Malay, Indonesian and a group containing texts written in a set of other languages. In Table 1 we can see how they are grouped according to their similarities. Groups A, C and F contain similar languages and groups B, D and E include language varieties. There are 18,000 training, 2,000 development and 1,000 test instances/sentences per language. In addition, the

Language groups	Unmodified texts (**Test set A**) **Skip-gram + LG (run1)**	**Skip-gram + SVM (run2)**	**SenVec + LG (run3)**	Named entities substituted with #NE# (**Test set B**) **Skip-gram + LG (run1)**	**Skip-gram + SVM (run2)**	**SenVec + LG (run3)**
Bulgarian	**1.000**	**1.000**	0.985	**1.000**	**1.000**	0.998
Macedonian	**1.000**	**1.000**	0.999	**1.000**	**1.000**	0.998
Overall (group A)	**1.000**	**1.000**	0.992	**1.000**	**1.000**	0.998
Bosnian	**0.803**	0.795	0.744	**0.751**	0.750	0.641
Croatian	**0.859**	0.837	0.847	**0.858**	0.853	0.769
Serbian	0.751	0.802	**0.912**	0.747	0.772	**0.871**
Overall (group B)	0.804	0.811	**0.834**	0.785	**0.791**	0.760
Czech	**0.999**	**0.999**	0.998	**1.000**	**1.000**	**1.000**
Slovak	**1.000**	**1.000**	0.993	**1.000**	**1.000**	0.951
Overall (group C)	**0.999**	**0.999**	0.995	**1.000**	**1.000**	0.976
Spanish (Spain)	0.821	**0.878**	0.863	0.806	**0.853**	0.796
Spanish (Argentina)	**0.903**	0.870	0.876	**0.847**	0.770	0.816
Overall (group D)	0.862	**0.874**	0.869	**0.826**	0.806	0.806
Portuguese (Brazil)	**0.945**	0.926	0.876	**0.904**	0.900	0.783
Portuguese (Portugal)	0.832	0.879	**0.900**	0.780	0.832	**0.866**
Overall (group E)	0.888	**0.902**	0.888	0.842	**0.866**	0.824
Malay	0.992	0.994	**0.998**	0.987	**0.990**	0.917
Indonesian	0.993	**0.996**	0.994	0.989	0.994	**0.996**
Overall (group F)	0.992	0.995	**0.996**	0.988	**0.992**	0.956
Other languages	**0.998**	**0.998**	**0.998**	**0.998**	**0.998**	**0.998**
Overall (all groups)	0.921	**0.927**	**0.927**	0.905	**0.908**	0.885

Table 1: Accuracy results in discrimination between similar languages using test set A and B.

dataset is provided in two variants. The test set A includes unmodified journalistic texts. Test set B used different instances and substituted named entities for the #NE# tag to study the bias they provide. Results measure the accuracy of language identification of the Skip-gram + LG, Skip-gram + SVM and SenVec + LG classifiers[2] in both datasets.

3.2 Results

As we can see in Table 1, similar languages were easier to distinguish, with accuracies close to 100%. A similar trend is appreciated to identify the "other languages" group, which contains instances of several alternative languages such as French or Catalan. The language varieties were more difficult, obtaining values in the range 80–90%, the most difficult being the group of the Serbo-Croatian language, followed by the Spanish and Portuguese. Regarding the substitution of named entities with the #NE# tag, we appreciated a small reduction in accuracy, more elevated for the SenVec model. In general, the differences between the models and classifiers were reduced. In Table 2 we can see the evaluation of statistical significance among the different models. SVM provided slight improvements (increasing several times the training time) with respect to the logistic classifier, and inferred more accurate frontiers among languages (see language variety group inner values). The Skip-gram approach was less sensitive to the substitution of named entities and offered the best performance in average. That model is a few points below compared to the best participant in the task which achieved 95.54% and 94.01% in the test set A and B respectively.

	R<#run> <(test set) {A,B}> **R1A**	**R2A**	**R3A**	**R1B**	**R2B**	**R3B**
R1A		=	=	*	*	*
R2A			=	*	*	*
R3A				*	*	*
R1B					=	*
R2B						*
R3B						

Table 2: Pairwise statistical test of significance among submitted runs (= not significant $p > 0.05$; * significant $0.05 \geq p > 0.01$).

Comparing the results with those obtained for language variety identification in Franco-Salvador et al. (2015), closer to 70%, with respect the previous experiments carried out on the HispaBlogs dataset we would like to highlight that: i) there is a further difficulty when processing noisy social media texts than more formal journalistic ones; ii) the length of the texts in HispaBlogs is of 10 posts for user blog (that could introduce ambiguity and

[2]We used 300-dimensional vectors, context windows of size 10, and 20 negative words for each sample. We used the word2vec toolkit to perform the phrase detection and the vector training:
`https://code.google.com/p/word2vec/`

noise) whereas in the DSLCC dataset is of a single sentence per instance; iii) the number of classes in HispaBlogs is five whereas in DSLCC is three per group in the worst case; and iv) we think that the overfitting may have a significant impact on the results: whereas in HispaBlogs a different author is given in each instance, in DSLCC there is no such restriction. Therefore, models may profile the author's writing style to classify the test instances of the same authors they already saw in the training set.

4 Conclusions

In this work we evaluated the Discriminating between similar languages 2015 shared task. We employed the continuous Skip-gram model to generate distributed representations of words and sentences with interesting insights about the identification of languages. As expected, groups of language varieties were more difficult to classify. In addition, the substitution of named entities with the #NE# tag slightly reduced the accuracy. Finally, the combination of word vectors (Skip-gram) offered better results on average than the use of directly generated vectors of sentences (SenVec). As future work we will investigate further how to apply distributed representations to other author profiling tasks. We will continue working also to improve the current model in order to generate better distributed representations for discriminating between similar languages.

Acknowledgments

This research has been carried out within the framework of the European Commission WIQ-EI IRSES (no. 269180) and DIANA - Finding Hidden Knowledge in Texts (TIN2012-38603-C02) projects, and the VLC/CAMPUS Microcluster on Multimodal Interaction in Intelligent Systems. The work of the third author was partially funded by Autoritas Consulting SA and by Spanish Ministry of Economics under grant ECOPORTUNITY IPT-2012-1220-430000.

References

Andrew G Barto. 1998. *Reinforcement learning: An introduction*. MIT press.

Simon Carter, Wouter Weerkamp, and Manos Tsagkias. 2013. Microblog language identification: Overcoming the limitations of short, unedited and idiomatic text. *Language Resources and Evaluation*, 47(1):195–215.

Chih-Chung Chang and Chih-Jen Lin. 2011. Libsvm: A library for support vector machines. *ACM Transactions on Intelligent Systems and Technology (TIST)*, 2(3):27.

Marc Franco-Salvador, Francisco Rangel, Paolo Rosso, Mariona Taulé, and M. Antònia Martí. 2015. Language variety identification using distributed representations of words and documents. In *Proceeding of the 6th International Conference of CLEF on Experimental IR meets Multilinguality, Multimodality, and Interaction (CLEF 2015)*, volume LNCS(9283). Springer-Verlag.

Thomas Gottron and Nedim Lipka. 2010. A comparison of language identification approaches on short, query-style texts. In *Advances in information retrieval*, pages 611–614. Springer.

Cyril Goutte, Serge Léger, and Marine Carpuat. 2014. The nrc system for discriminating similar languages. In *Proceedings of the First Workshop on Applying NLP Tools to Similar Languages, Varieties and Dialects*, pages 139–145, Dublin, Ireland, August. Association for Computational Linguistics.

Michael U. Gutmann and Aapo Hyvärinen. 2012. Noise-contrastive estimation of unnormalized statistical models, with applications to natural image statistics. *The Journal of Machine Learning Research*, 13(1):307–361.

Quoc V. Le and Tomas Mikolov. 2014. Distributed representations of sentences and documents. In *Proceedings of the 31st International Conference on Machine Learning*.

Wolfgang Maier and Carlos Gómez-Rodríguez. 2014. Language variety identification in spanish tweets. In *Proceedings of the EMNLP'2014 Workshop on Language Technology for Closely Related Languages and Language Variants*, pages 25–35, Doha, Qatar, October. Association for Computational Linguistics.

Paul McNamee. 2005. Language identification: a solved problem suitable for undergraduate instruction. *Journal of Computing Sciences in Colleges*, 20(3):94–101.

Tomas Mikolov, Kai Chen, Greg Corrado, and Jeffrey Dean. 2013a. Efficient estimation of word representations in vector space. In *Proceedings of Workshop at International Conference on Learning Representations*.

Tomas Mikolov, Ilya Sutskever, Kai Chen, Greg S Corrado, and Jeff Dean. 2013b. Distributed representations of words and phrases and their compositionality. In *Advances in Neural Information Processing Systems 26*, pages 3111–3119.

Andriy Mnih and Yee Whye Teh. 2012. A fast and simple algorithm for training neural probabilistic language models. *arXiv preprint arXiv:1206.6426*.

Frederic Morin and Yoshua Bengio. 2005. Hierarchical probabilistic neural network language model. In *Proceedings of the international workshop on artificial intelligence and statistics*, pages 246–252. Citeseer.

Francisco Rangel and Paolo Rosso. 2015. On the impact of emotions on author profiling. *Information Processing & Management*, pages n/a, DOI: 10.1016/j.ipm.2015.06.003 (In press).

Francisco Rangel, Paolo Rosso, Moshe Moshe Koppel, Efstathios Stamatatos, and Giacomo Inches. 2013. Overview of the author profiling task at pan 2013. In *Forner P., Navigli R., Tufis D. (Eds.), CLEF 2013 Labs and Workshops, Notebook Papers*, volume 1179, pages 352–365. CEUR-WS.org.

Francisco Rangel, Paolo Rosso, Irina Chugur, Martin Potthast, Martin Trenkmann, Benno Stein, Ben Verhoeven, and Walter Daelemans. 2014. Overview of the 2nd author profiling task at pan 2014. In *Cappellato L., Ferro N., Halvey M., Kraaij W. (Eds.) CLEF 2014 Labs and Workshops, Notebook Papers.*, volume 1180, pages 898–827. CEUR-WS.org.

Fatiha Sadat, Farnazeh Kazemi, and Atefeh Farzindar. 2014. Automatic identification of arabic language varieties and dialects in social media. In *Proceeding of the 1st. International Workshop on Social Media Retrieval and Analysis SoMeRa*.

Liling Tan, Marcos Zampieri, Nikola Ljubešic, and Jörg Tiedemann. 2014. Merging comparable data sources for the discrimination of similar languages: The dsl corpus collection. In *Proceedings of the 7th Workshop on Building and Using Comparable Corpora*, pages 11–15, Reykjavik, Iceland.

Marcos Zampieri and Binyam Gebrekidan Gebre. 2012. Automatic identification of language varieties: The case of portuguese. In *KONVENS2012-The 11th Conference on Natural Language Processing*, pages 233–237. Österreichischen Gesellschaft für Artificial Intelligende (ÖGAI).

Marcos Zampieri, Liling Tan, Nikola Ljubešić, and Jörg Tiedemann. 2014. A report on the dsl shared task 2014. In *Proceedings of the First Workshop on Applying NLP Tools to Similar Languages, Varieties and Dialects*, pages 58–67, Dublin, Ireland, August. Association for Computational Linguistics.

Marcos Zampieri, Liling Tan, Nikola Ljubešić, Jörg Tiedemann, and Preslav Nakov. 2015. Overview of the dsl shared task 2015. In *Proceedings of the Joint Workshop on Language Technology for Closely Related Languages, Varieties and Dialects (LT4VarDial)*, Hissar, Bulgaria.

Arkaitz Zubiaga, Inaki San Vicente, Pablo Gamallo, José Ramom Pichel, Inaki Alegria, Nora Aranberri, Aitzol Ezeiza, and Vıctor Fresno. 2014. Overview of tweetlid: Tweet language identification at sepln 2014. *TweetLID@ SEPLN*.

Joint Bayesian Morphology learning for Dravidian languages

Arun Kumar
Universitat Oberta de Catalunya
akallararajappan@uoc.edu

Lluís Padró
Universitat Politècnica de Catalunya
padro@cs.upc.edu

Antoni Oliver
Universitat Oberta de Catalunya
aoliverg@uoc.edu

Abstract

In this paper a methodology for learning the complex agglutinative morphology of some Indian languages using Adaptor Grammars and morphology rules is presented. Adaptor grammars are a compositional Bayesian framework for grammatical inference, where we define a morphological grammar for agglutinative languages and morphological boundaries are inferred from a plain text corpus. Once morphological segmentations are produce, regular expressions for sandhi rules and orthography are applied to achieve the final segmentation. We test our algorithm in the case of two complex languages from the Dravidian family. The same morphological model and results are evaluated comparing to other state-of-the art unsupervised morphology learning systems.

1 Introduction

Morphemes are the smallest individual units that form words. For example, the Malayalam word (മലകളുടെ, `malakaḷuṭe`, related to mountains) consists of several morphemes (stem `mala`, plural marker `kal`, and genitive case marker `uṭe`). Morphological segmentation is one of the most studied tasks in unsupervised morphology learning (Hammarström and Borin, 2011). In unsupervised morphology learning, the words are segmented into corresponding morphemes with any supervision, as for example morphological annotations. It provides the simplest form of morphological analysis for languages that lack supervised knowledge or annotation. In agglutinative languages, there is a close connection between suffixes and morpho-syntactic functions and thus, in those languages the morphological segmentation may approximate morphological analysis well enough. Most unsupervised morphological segmentation systems have been developed and tested on a small set of European languages (Creutz and Lagus, 2007a), mainly English, Finnish and Turkish, with few exceptions in Semitic languages (Poon et al., 2009). These languages show a variety of morphological complexities, including inflection, agglutination and compounding. However, when applying those systems on other language groups with their own morphological complexities, we cannot expect the good results demonstrated so far to be automatically ported into those languages. We assume that morphological similarities of same language family enable us to define a general model that work across all languages of the family.

In this paper we work with a set of Indian languages that are highly agglutinated, with words consisting of a root and a sequence of possibly many morphemes and with each suffix corresponding to a morpho-syntactic function such as case, number, aspect, mood or gender. In addition to that, they are highly and productively compounding, allowing the formation of very long words incorporating several concepts. Thus, the morphological segmentation in those languages may partially look like a word segmentation task, which attempts to split the words in a sentence.

Dravidian languages (Steever, 2003) are a group of Indian languages that shows extensive use of morpho-phonological changes in word or morpheme boundaries during concatenation, a process called *sandhi*. This process also occurs in European languages (Andersen, 1986), but it becomes more important in the case of Dravidian languages as they use alpha-syllabic writing systems. (Taylor and Olson, 1995).

Recently, interest has shifted into semi-supervised morphological segmentation that enables to bias the model towards a certain language by using a small amount of annotated training data. We also adopt semi-supervised learning to more effectively deal with the complex orthography

Proceedings of the Joint Workshop on Language Technology for Closely Related Languages, Varieties and Dialects, pages 17–23,
Hissar, Bulgaria, September 10, 2015.

of the Dravidian languages. We use the Adaptor Grammars framework (Johnson et al., 2007a) for implementing our segmentation models that has been shown to be effective for semi-supervised morphological segmentation learning (Sirts and Goldwater, 2013) and it provides a computational platform for building Bayesian non-parametric models and its inference procedure. We learn the segmentation patterns from transliterated input and convert the segmented transliterations into the orthographic representation by applying a set of regular expressions created from morphological and orthographic rules to deal with *sandhi*.

We test our system on two major languages from the Dravidian family— Malayalam and Kannada. These languages, regardless of their large number of speakers, can be considered resource-scarce, for which not much annotated data available for building morphological analyzer. We build a model that makes use of languages morphological and orthographic similarities. In Section 2, we list them main morphological and orthographic similarities of these languages.

The structure of this paper is as follows. In Section 2 we describe more thoroughly the morphological and orthographic challenges presented in Dravidian languages. Section 3 describes the Adaptor Grammars framework. In section 4, we describe the morphological segmentation system for the Dravidian languages. Experimental setup is specified in Section 5, followed by the results and analysis in section 6 and conclusions in Section 7.

2 Morphology of Dravidian languages

In this study we focus on Kannada and Malayalam, which are two major languages in the south Dravidian group. These languages are inflected and highly agglutinative, which make them morphologically complex. The writing systems of these languages are alpha-syllabic, i.e. each symbol represents a syllable. In this section we discuss morphological and orthographic similarities of these languages in detail.

2.1 Orthography

Kannada and Malayalam follow an alpha-syllabic writing system in which individual symbols are syllables. In both languages symbols are called `akṣara`. The atomic symbols are classified into two main categories (`svaraṁ`, vowels) and (`vyaṅṅajnaṁ`, consonants). Both languages have fourteen vowels, (including `a, ā, i, ī, u, ū, e, ē, ai, o, ō, au, aṁ`)[1], where `aṁ` is an `anusvāram`, which means nasalized vowel. Table 1 shows some examples of their orthographic representation. These vowels are in atomic form but when they are combined with consonant symbols, the vowel symbols change to ligatures, resulting in consonant ligatures (see examples in Table 2).

Table 1: Vowels

ISO Transliteration	a	i	o	u
Malayalam	അ	ഇ	ഒ	ഉ
Kannada	ಅ	ಇ	ಈ	ಉ

Table 2: Consonant ligature

	Consonant	Vowel	Ligature
ISO Transliteration	m	ī	mī
Malayalam	മ	ഈ	മീ
Kannada	ಮ	ಈ	ಮೀ

Orthography of both languages supports a large number of compound characters resulting from the combination of two consonants symbols, as those shown in Table 3.

Table 3: Compound characters

ISO Transliteration	cca	kka
Malayalam	ച്ച	ക്ക
Kannada	ಚ್ಚ	ಕ್ಕ

The orthographic systems contain characters for numerals and Arabic numerals are also present in the system. See examples in table 4

2.2 Sandhi changes

Sandhi is a morpho-phonemic change happening in the morpheme or word boundaries at the time of concatenation. Both Kannada and Malayalam have three major kinds of *sandhi* formations: deletion, insertion and assimilation. In the case of deletion *sandhi*, when two syllables are joined together one of the syllable is deleted from the resulting combination, while insertion *sandhi* adds one syllable when two syllables are joined together. The *sandhi* formations found in Sanskrit are also found in these languages as these languages loan large

[1] These symbols are according to ISO romanization standard: ISO-15919

Table 4: Numerals

Arabic Numerals	1	2
Malayalam	൧	൨
Kannada	೧	೨

number of roots from Sanskrit. There are language specific sandhi, such as `visarga` sandhi. `Visarga` sandhi is commonly found in the case of loaned words from Sanskrit. `Visarga` is an allophone of phonemes /r/ and /s/ at the end of the utterance. Kannada orthography keeps the symbol for `visarga` but Malayalam orthography uses column symbol for representing it. As languages follow alpha-syllabic orthography, these *sandhi* changes will change the orthography of the resulting word, examples are listed in Table 5. In the examples, when the Malayalam stem `ma<u>l</u>a` (mountain) joined to āṇ (is), a new syllable y introduced to resulting word `ma<u>l</u>ayāṇ`. Similarly in the case of Kannada stem `magu`, when joined with `annu`, the resulting word `maguyannu` also includes an extra syllable y. These similarities between languages enable us to define a generic finite-state traducer for orthographic changes that are caused by phonological changes. An example of created rule for addition of syllabley is that when (`a`) is preceded with (`u`) and (`a`) a new syllable is y is added with resulting word.

Table 5: Sandhi Changes

Language	Insertion sandhi
Malayalam	`ma<u>l</u>a+āṇ` → `ma<u>l</u>ayāṇ`
Kannada	`Magu+annu` → `maguyannu`

2.3 Morphology

Due to those orthographic properties of Dravidian languages, morpheme boundaries are marked at the syllabic level. However, during concatenation, phonological changes *sandhi* may occur, so that the resulting word has a different orthography than the individual segments concatenated together. That means the surface form may be different from the lexical form. For example, in Malayalam the surface form of the word കണ്ടില്ല (`kaṇṭilla`) corresponds to the lexical form കണ്ടു + ഇല്ല (`kaṇṭu` + `illa`). The changes in orthography in surface form when lexical units are combined are present in this example. Kannada also exhibits similar properties.

Malayalam and Kannada use case markers for nominative, accusative, genitive, dative, instrumental, locative, and sociative (Agesthialingom and Gowda, 1976). In both languages, nouns inflect with gender, number, and case. Gender is marked for masculine and feminine, while neuter corresponds to the absence of gender marker. There are two categories of number markers: singular and plural. Both languages can use plural markers for showing respect. For example, the Kannada word (ವಾಯು `vāyu` wind) is inflected with masculine gender marker. Similarly, the Malayalam word (വായു `vāyu` wind) has a masculine gender marker. In the case of verb morphology, both languages inflect with tenses, mood, and aspect. Where mood can follow arative, subjunctive, conditional, imperative, presumptive , abilitative, and habitual. Aspect markers can follow three categories, such as simple, progressive, purposive. For example, the Kannada sentence (ನಾನು ಬಂದು `Nānu bandu` I come), the verb `bandu` inflected with present tense marker `u`. Similarly the Malayalam sentence (താരം വന്നു `tāraṁ vannu` Star comes), the verb `vannu` inflected with `u`, which is the present tense marker.

Compounding acts as another challenge in Dravidian languages where words can have a recursive compound structure. There can be compounds embedded in a compound word, which itself can become another compound (Mohanan, 1986). For instance, in Malayalam (`jātimātaviduveṣaṅṅaḷ`, hatred of caste and religion) consist of first compound (`jāti + māta`, caste and religion), joined with other compound (`viduveṣam`, hatred) and plural inflection `ṅṅaḷ`.

3 Adaptor Grammars

Adaptor Grammars (AG) (Johnson et al., 2007a) is a non-parametric Bayesian framework for performing grammatical inference over parse trees. AG has two components—a PCFG (Probabilistic Context Free Grammar) and an adaptor function. The PCFG specifies the grammar rules used to generate the data. The adaptor function transforms the probabilities of the generated parse trees so that the probabilities of the adapted parse trees may be substantially larger than under the conditionally independent PCFG model. Various Bayesian nonparametric models can be used as Adaptor function, such as HDP (Teh et al., 2006). For instance, the Pitman-Yor Adaptor (Johnson et al., 2007a), which is also used in this work, transforms the probability of an adapted parse tree in such a way that it is proportional to the number of times this tree has been observed elsewhere in the data. We provide an informal description of adaptor grammar here. An adaptor grammar consists of terminals V and non-terminals N, (including a start symbol, S), and initial rule set R with probability p, like a Probabilistic Context Free Grammar (PCFG). A non-terminal $A \in N$, has got a vector of concentration parameters α, where $\alpha_A > 0$. Then we say non-terminal A is adapted. If $\alpha_A = 0$ then A is an unadapted non-terminal. A non-terminal A, which is unadpted expand as in PCFG but an adapted non-terminal A can expand in two ways:

1. A can expand to a subtree t with probability $n_t/n_A + \alpha_A$, where n_t is the number of times A has expanded to t before and
2. Expand as in PCFG considering the probability propositional to concentration parameter α_A

Inference on this model can achieved using a sampling procedure . The formal definition of AGs can be found in (Johnson et al., 2007a), details of the inference procedures are described in (Johnson et al., 2007b) and (Johnson and Goldwater, 2009).

4 AGs for morphological segmentation for Dravidian languages

Dravidian languages are highly agglutinative, which means that a stem can be attached a sequence of several suffixes and several words can be concatenated together to form compounds. The segmentation model has to take these language properties into account.

We can define a grammar reflecting the agglutinative structure of language similar to the compounding grammar of (Sirts and Goldwater, 2013), excluding prefixes:

$$\begin{aligned} \text{Word} &\rightarrow \underline{\text{Compound}}^{+} \\ \underline{\text{Compound}} &\rightarrow \underline{\text{Stem}}\ \underline{\text{Suffix}}^{*} \\ \underline{\text{Stem}} &\rightarrow \underline{\text{SubMorphs}}^{+} \\ \underline{\text{Suffix}} &\rightarrow \underline{\text{SubMorphs}}^{+} \end{aligned} \tag{1}$$

Segmentation of long agglutinated sentences is the aim of above described grammar, where we consider that words are composed of words[2] and words can be composed of Stem and Suffix, where Stem and Suffix are adapted non terminals, which are "adapted" with Pitman-Yor Process (Pitman and Yor, 1997). Both Stem and Suffix can generated from drawing of Pitman-Yor process or by following PCFG rule. If these non-terminals expand according to PCFG rule, it expand to *Submorphs*, which is an intermediate levels added before terminals, For more details refer (Sirts and Goldwater, 2013)

[2]The word "compound" is used in our representation for words

The *Submorphs* can be defined in the following way

$$\begin{aligned} \text{Submorphs} &\rightarrow \text{Submorph} \\ \text{Submorphs} &\rightarrow \text{Submorph Submorphs} \\ \text{Submorphs} &\rightarrow \text{Chars} \\ \text{Chars} &\rightarrow \text{Char} \\ \text{Chars} &\rightarrow \text{CharChars} \end{aligned} \tag{2}$$

The Submorphs can be composed of single morph or Submorhs, which are combinations of Char. In our case Char is our internal representation for alpha-syllabic characters. The above grammar can generate various parse trees as a we put a Pitman-Yor prior on component. It is going to produce most probable morphological segmentation based on the prior probabilities. For more details of this procedure, refer (Johnson and Goldwater, 2009)

This grammar enables representing long agglutinated phrases that are common in Dravidian languages. For instance, an agglutinated Malayalam word phrase `sansthānaṅṅaḷileānnāṉ` with the correct morphological segmentation `sansth` + `ānaṅṅaḷileā` + `nnāṉ` can be represented using the grammar.

Although this grammar uses the knowledge about the agglutinative nature of the language, it is otherwise knowledge-free because it doesn't model the specific morphotactic regularities of the particular language. Next, we experiment with grammars that are specifically tailored for Dravidian languages and express the specific morphotactic patterns found in those languages. We look at the regular morphological templates described in linguistic textbooks (Krishnamurti, 1976) and (Steever, 2003) rather than generating just a sequence of generic Suffixes.

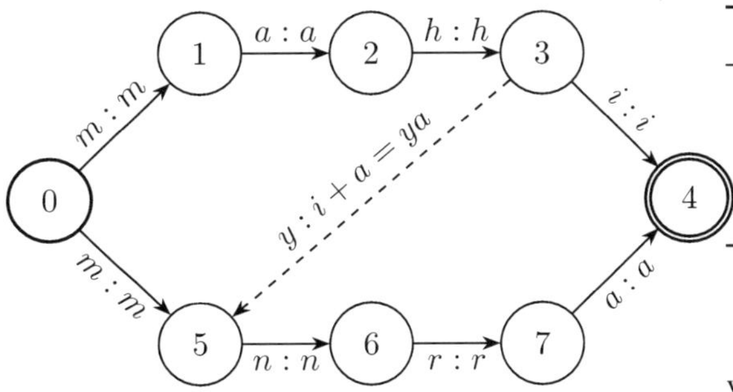

Figure 1: Example of sandhi rule in FST

4.1 Dealing with Sandhi

As explained above, the words in Dravidian languages often undergo phonological changes when morphemes or compound parts are concatenated together. Thus, in order to correctly express the segmented words in script, it is necessary to model those changes properly.

In this work we deal with *sandhi* during a post-processing step where we apply to the segmented words a set of regular expression rules that describe the valid *sandhi* rules. Our approach is similar to (Vempaty and Nagalla, 2011) where rules for orthographic changes are created. However, we use FST rules at the syllable level. Our method works with a general phonetic notation, which is the same for both languages. For example, the Malayalam word (marannaḷ, trees) is combination of (maram tree + nnal plural marker). We create a context sensitive rule for the orthographic change, which look like $V \rightarrow V$ m"+"||nnal. In the above V is set of all syllables in the languages. The same rule also stands for Kannada orthographic change. Similarly we create rule for orthographic changes due to *sandhi*. One example of finite-state transducer rule to handle addition sandhi is given in figure 1. It handles the ya sandhi happens change during the insertion sandhi. We have 62 rules for Malayalam and 34 rules for Kannada for handling sandhi changes. The statistics of the data is shown in 5.

5 Data and Experiments

We conduct our experiments on word lists extracted from Wikipedia and newspaper's websites. The statistics of the data sets are given in Table 6. Word list consist of 30 million tokens of Kannada and 40 million tokens of Malayalam. The data set consist of named entities, proper names and abbreviations. We also have 10k morphologically hand-segmented words, which act as our gold standard file.

	Kannada	Malayalam
Token frequency	30M	40M
Types	1M	1M
Labeled	10k	10k
RE Rules	62	34

Table 6: Statistics of the data sets.

In order to deal with complex orthographies of Kannada and Malayalam, we have created a internal representation, which is unique for both languages. The conversion was done in following way: the Malayalam word (അതേസമയം , atēsamayam) converted in to *a t h e s a m y a m*. During this process complex ligatures are converted into corresponding extended ASCII format and put spaces between the characters. Similarly a Kannada word (ಮಧ್ಯದ, madhyada) converted to *m a d y a d a*. This representation allow us to use the same grammar for both languages. The conversion of orthographic form to internal representation is as follows. In the first step we have converted language's scripts to corresponding ISO romanization. This representation helps in getting unique values for various ligatures and compound characters. Once the script is converted to ISO romanized form, we convert it into Extended ASCII form with unique values for each characters. As part of our experiment, we converted all words in the lists and morphological segmentations to our internal representation. For training the AG models[3], we use the scenarios proposed by (Sirts and Goldwater, 2013) we train the models using 10K, 20K 40k, 50K, 80K most frequent word types in each language with same grammar and segment the test data inductively with a parser using the AG posterior grammar as the trained model. We run five independent experiments with each setting for 1000 iterations after which we collect a single sample for getting the AG posterior grammar.

Using the trained models we segment our gold standard. Once the AG posterior grammar produce the morphological segmentation in internal form we converted internal representation into corresponding orthographic form for evaluation of result. The process of converting the internal repre-

[3]Software available at `http://web.science.mq.edu.au/~mjohnson/`

sentation to orthographic form is as follows. We take the internal representation of a word one by one and we apply finite-state rule that takes care of *sandhi* and then it convert back to orthography. The number of finite-state rules, is listed as RE rules in the Table 5.

6 Evaluation, Error analysis and Discussion

The evaluation is based on how well the methods predicts the morpheme boundaries in orthographic form and calculates precision, recall and F- score. We used Python suite provided in the morpho-challenge website[4] for evaluation purposes We also train Morfessor baseline, Morfessor-CAP and Undivide, with 80K word types. We compare our results with several baselines that have been previously successfully used for agglutinated languages: Finnish and Turkish. For unsupervised baselines we use Morfessor Categories-MAP (Creutz and Lagus, 2007b) and Undivide (Dasgupta and Ng, 2007). We train Morfessor Categories-MAP with the 80K most frequent word types and produce a model. Using this model the gold standard file is segmented and the results are compared with the manual segmentations. The same process is carried out in the case of Morfessor baseline. In the case of Undivide, we apply the system on the gold standard file and get the segmentation. We use Undivide software because it performed very well in the case of highly inflected Indian language Bengali. The results are evaluated by computing the segment boundary F1 score (F1) as is standard for morphological segmentation task.

The result achieved is presented in the table 7. In the table (P) stands for Precision and (R) stands for Recall and (F) stands for F-score.

On the manual analysis of the predicted word segmentations by our system and other baselines, we note the following:

- Our system was able to identify the sandhi changes and orthographic changes due to sandhi but other systems were unable to do that because of lack knowledge of orthography and sandhi changes.

- In the case of compound characters, Morfessor, Morfessor- MAP and Undivide segmented it into two constituent character, which is not required. For example, the Malayalam character (ങ്ക, nka) to (n) and (ka).

- All algorithms have divided compounds words.

We did not evaluated the result produced by the Adaptor Grammar individually as we need the output in language's script.

7 Conclusion and future research

We have presented a semi-supervised morphology learning technique that uses statistical measures and linguistic rules. The result of the proposed method outperforms other state-of-art unsupervised morphology learning techniques. The major contribution of this paper is the use of same model of morphology for segmenting two morphologically complex languages and the *sandhi* changes in both the languages are handled using a single finite-state transducer. In essence, we can consider it as a hybrid system, which make use of statistical information and linguistic rules together to produce better results. The experiments show that morphology of two complex languages can be learned jointly. Other important aspect of these experiments is that we tested Adaptor Grammars in the case of complex Indian languages and showed that it can be used in languages with complex morphology and orthography. The major aim of the study was to show a general model of morphology, which could be used to learn morphology of two languages. As further research, we intend to train the system with larger number of tokens and evaluate the performance in the presence of large amount of data. As we also noted an improvement in the performance when the number of word type increases.

Acknowledgments

We thank the anonymous reviewers for their careful reading of our manuscript and their many insightfulcomments and suggestions.

References

Shanmugam Agesthialingom and K Kushalappa Gowda. 1976. *Dravidian case system*. Number 39. Annamalai University.

Henning Andersen. 1986. *Sandhi phenomena in the languages of Europe*, volume 33. Walter de Gruyter.

[4]http://research.ics.aalto.fi/events/morphochallenge/

Method	Kannada			Malayalam		
	P	R	F	P	R	F
Undivide	40.98	47.17	43.86	64.08	27.12	38.22
Morfessor-base	67.92	59.02	45.63	38.21	41.59	48.54
Morfessor-MAP	70.32	53.77	62.1	62.64	47.11	53.77
Adaptor Grammar	73.63	59.82	66.01	65.66	54.32	59.45

Table 7: Results for several systems

Mathias Creutz and Krista Lagus. 2007a. Unsupervised models for morpheme segmentation and morphology learning. *ACM Transactions on Speech and Language Processing (TSLP)*, 4(1):3.

Mathias Creutz and Krista Lagus. 2007b. Unsupervised models for morpheme segmentation and morphology learning. *ACM Transactions on Speech and Language Processing*, 4(1):3:1–3:34.

Sajib Dasgupta and Vincent Ng. 2007. High-performance, language-independent morphological segmentation. In *HLT-NAACL*, pages 155–163.

Harald Hammarström and Lars Borin. 2011. Unsupervised learning of morphology. *Computational Linguistics*, 37(2):309–350.

Mark Johnson and Sharon Goldwater. 2009. Improving nonparametric Bayesian inference: Experiments on unsupervised word segmentation with Adaptor Grammars. In *naacl09*, pages 317–325.

Mark Johnson, Thomas L. Griffiths, and Sharon Goldwater. 2007a. Adaptor Grammars: a framework for specifying compositional nonparametric Bayesian models. In *Advances in Neural Information Processing Systems 19*, pages 641–648.

Mark Johnson, Thomas L. Griffiths, and Sharon Goldwater. 2007b. Bayesian inference for PCFGs via Markov chain Monte Carlo. In *HLT-NAACL*, pages 139–146.

Bhadriraju Krishnamurti. 1976. Comparative dravidian studies. *Current Trends in Linguistics: Index*, 14:309.

Karuvannur P Mohanan. 1986. The theory of lexical phonology: Studies in natural language and linguistic theory. *Dordrecht: D. Reidel.*

Jim Pitman and Marc Yor. 1997. The two-parameter poisson-dirichlet distribution derived from a stable subordinator. *The Annals of Probability*, pages 855–900.

Hoifung Poon, Colin Cherry, and Kristina Toutanova. 2009. Unsupervised morphological segmentation with log-linear models. In *Proceedings of Human Language Technologies: The 2009 Annual Conference of the North American Chapter of the Association for Computational Linguistics*, pages 209–217. Association for Computational Linguistics.

Kairit Sirts and Sharon Goldwater. 2013. Minimally-supervised morphological segmentation using adaptor grammars. *Transactions of the Association for Computational Linguistics*, 1:255–266.

Sanford B Steever. 2003. *The Dravidian Languages*. Routledge.

Insup Taylor and David R Olson. 1995. *Scripts and literacy: Reading and learning to read alphabets, syllabaries, and characters*, volume 7. Springer Science & Business Media.

Yee Whye Teh, Michael I Jordan, Matthew J Beal, and David M Blei. 2006. Hierarchical dirichlet processes. *Journal of the american statistical association*, 101(476).

Phani Chaitanya Vempaty and Satish Chandra Prasad Nagalla. 2011. Automatic sandhi spliting method for telugu, an indian language. *Procedia-Social and Behavioral Sciences*, 27:218–225.

Use of Transformation-Based Learning in Annotation Pipeline of Igbo, an African Language.

Ikechukwu Onyenwe[1], **Mark Hepple**[1], **Chinedu Uchechukwu**[2], **and Ignatius Ezeani**[1]
[1]Department of Computer Science, University of Sheffield, UK
{i.onyenwe, m.r.hepple, ignatius.ezeani}@sheffield.ac.uk
[2]Department of Linguistics, Nnamdi Azikiwe University, Nigeria
neduchi@yahoo.com

Abstract

The accuracy of an annotated corpus can be increased through evaluation and revision of the annotation scheme, and through adjudication of the disagreements found. In this paper, we describe a novel process that has been applied to improve a part-of-speech (POS) tagged corpus for the African language Igbo.
An inter-annotation agreement (IAA) exercise was undertaken to iteratively revise the tagset used in the creation of the initial tagged corpus, with the aim of refining the tagset and maximizing annotator performance. The tagset revisions and other corrections were efficiently propagated to the overall corpus in a semi-automated manner using transformation-based learning (TBL) to identify candidates for correction and to propose possible tag corrections. The affected word-tag pairs in the corpus were inspected to ensure a high quality end-product with an accuracy that would not be achieved through a purely automated process. The results show that the tagging accuracy increases from 88% to 94%. The tagged corpus is potentially re-usable for other dialects of the language.

1 Introduction

When texts and human judgements are stored in computer-readable form, the result is called annotation. Annotation is developed mostly through hand-coded means, so it is important to measure the reliability of the tagset that produced it. The fundamental assumption of this exercise, as discussed in (Artstein and Massimo, 2007; Raquel, 2011), is that the output of manual annotation is considered reliable if it can be computed that annotators are consistent, and the consistency is measured using metrics from the study of Landis and Koch (1977), Krippendorff (1980), and Green (1997). If different annotators produce consistently similar results then we can infer that they have internalized a similar understanding of the tagging scheme, and can expect them to perform consistently under this understanding. The outcome of this exercise is high consistency tagged sub-corpora containing POS-tags described in the tagset.

This paper describes how we leveraged the by-products of the inter-annotation agreement (IAA) exercise to improve the quality of the initial tagged Igbo corpus (ITC0), instead of ignoring them and tagging new text, which saves effort, time and money. A quality tagged corpus can help to maximize the performance of automatic POS-taggers used for tagging similar texts. We employ both manual and automatic processes in a semi-automatic method for this work. Our semi-automatic annotation method uses Transformation-based Learning (TBL) and a human expert, who is involved in several stages of the process. First, an initial Igbo tagged corpus (ITC0) was developed in a distributed manner using the tagset reported in Onyenwe et al., (2014). Through an inter-annotation agreement (IAA) exercise, this tagset (TS0) was evaluated and revised to ensure a more reliable and reproducible result. Then we use TBL to find and propagate changes from the IAA to this initial tagged corpus in an automated manner; an expert human annotator verifies locations TBL has marked for changes instead going through the entire text. Through this semi-automated process, the quality of the tagged corpus is increased with minimum expense. TBL is suitable for this because its inductive method performs very well using annotated corpora whose sizes are smaller than that of n-gram models, and it is an error-driven learner.

Proceedings of the Joint Workshop on Language Technology for Closely Related Languages, Varieties and Dialects, pages 24–33,
Hissar, Bulgaria, September 10, 2015. ©2015 Association for Computational Linguistics

TBL is a machine learning (ML) algorithm originally developed by Brill (1992). It starts with an initial state and requires a correctly tagged text, called *truth*, for training. The training process iteratively acquires an ordered list of rules that correct the errors found in the initial state until this initial state resembles the truth to some acceptable degree.

2 The Igbo Language

Igbo is one of the major languages spoken in eastern Nigeria by about 32 million native speakers[1]. It has been classified as a Benue-Congo language of the Kwa sub-group of the Niger-Congo family[2]. It adopts the Ọnwụ Committee orthography[3] and has 28 consonants and 8 vowels. Nine of the consonants are digraphs and the vowels are divided into two harmony groups that are distinguished on the basis of the Advanced Tongue Root (ATR) phenomenon (Uchechukwu, 2008). The majority of the words of the language select their vowels from the same harmony group. There are 3 distinct tones recognized in the language, *High* [´], *Low* [`], *downstep* [¯] (Emenanjo, 1978; Ikekeonwu, 1999). The tonal features of the language could be lexical or grammatical. For example, at the word level, *akwa* could mean 'bed/bridge', 'cry', 'cloth', or 'egg', but can be disambiguated with tones, as follows: akwa "cry", akwà "cloth", àkwà "bed or brigde", àkwa "egg". At the grammatical level, an interrogative sentence is distinguished from a declarative sentence through a change in tone (e.g. *ọ ga-abịa* "He will come", *ọ̀ ga-abịa?* "Will he come?"). Igbo is an agglutinative language in which its lexical categories undergo affixation, especially the verbs, to form a lexical unit. For example, *ericharịrị* in word form is made up of 4 morphemes: the verbal vowel prefix "e", verb root "ri", extensional suffix "cha", and a second extensional suffix "rịrị". Its occurrence in the sentence *"Obi must eat up that food"* is illustrated below:

Obi	ga-ericharịrị	nri	ahụ
Obi	aux-eat.completely.must	food	DET

[1] http://en.wikipedia.org/wiki/Igbo_people [July, 2015]

[2] http://www.igboguide.org/HT-igbogrammar.htm [July, 2015]

[3] http://www.columbia.edu/itc/mealac/pritchett/00fwp/igbo/txt_onwu_1961.pdf [July, 2015]

Igbo word order is Subject-Verb-Object (SVO), with a complement to the right of the head in all types of phrases, for example, *"Okeke killed a snake"* is written:

Okeke	gbu-ru	agwọ
Okeke	kill-rV(Past)	snake

3 Related Work

Finding and correcting errors to make more accurate annotated data as found in Loftsson (2009) and Helgadóttir et al., (2012) and our work are relatively similar in the aspect of inspecting marked data positions, but entirely different in methods. Loftsson (2009) and Helgadóttir et al., (2012) applied trained POS-taggers singly and combined, respectively, then the outputs were compared with the gold standard and differences found were marked as error candidates for verification. Whereas our method projects changes made in the IAA into the main tagged corpus, and all positions where these changes occurred are inspected further.

4 Building Input States of TBL

TBL makes use of two input states in its contextual module: the initial state and the truth state. Sections 4.1 and 4.2 describe these two input states.

4.1 Corpus Creation and Annotations

The Igbo language resources used for this study are the New World Translation Bible[4] (NWT) and the initial tagset (TS0) described in Onyenwe et al., (2014). For this study, we collected the new testament portion, which is about 260k tokens and 8k sentences. For rapid POS-tagging, chapters in the Bible corpus were allocated randomly to six groups, producing six corpora portions of approximately 45,000 tokens each (see table 1); each annotator annotates one group separately. The resulting output of this shared task is ITC0.

Key features of the initial tagset used to produce ITC0 comprise two parts, 44 POS-tags for non inflected tokens and 15 for inflected tokens. These 15 POS-tags are represented as α_XS for $\alpha \in \{$infinitive verbs, simple verbs, participles, gerunds, auxiliaries, conjunctions, interrogatives, $\ldots\}$ and _XS for any affixes, and without _XS are collapsed in the 44 POS-tags. The reason behind

[4] Obtained from jw.org.

Group 1	*Matthew, Philemon, 2 Peter, 1 Timothy, 1 Peter*
Group 2	*Acts, 2 Corinthians*
Group 3	*Mark, Revelation, Galatians, 3 John, 2 John*
Group 4	*John, Philipians, James, Colossians, 1 John, 1 Thessalonians*
Group 5	*Luke, Ephessians, 2 Thessalonians, Titus*
Group 6	*Romans, Hebrew, 1 Corinthians, 2 Timothy, Jude*

Table 1: Bible Book Selections by Group

this division is to capture all tokens with and without affixes in the main corpus since Igbo is an agglutinative language, which is a valuable step towards automated morphological segmentation of Igbo. Also found in this TS0 is multiword cases in the nominal class, which is caused by verb nominalization and its inherent complement. Special tags are used to represent this: tags for the verbal and inherent components.

4.1.1 Cleaning the Corpus "ITC0"

Given the six POS-tagged sub-corpora, we collected the best examples and eliminated errors found in the process. In most cases, this process is indistinguishable from "editing". The types of errors found are ambiguous-tag (1st row of table 10; where annotators could not apply a specific POS-tag to a particular token), no-tag (2nd and 3rd rows of table 10; where tokens are not classified by annotators) and wrong-form (4th row of table 10; where valid POS-tags are wrongly represented). POS-tags found in this error set are 39 in number and 5,062 tokens were affected (1.92% of the main corpus). Proper consultations were made with an Igbo linguist to resolve errors in the unspecified-tag and no-tag sets. In solving the remainder, we built a POS-tag replacement dictionary of the errors in the wrong-form class and pass the ITC0 through it to produce ITC1. The POS-tag replacement dictionary is represented as

tag_replacement = {'INT':'INTJ', 'VSI_OVS': 'VSI_XS', ...}

Another issue that caused no-tag error was improper word form. For example, the token *bụla* is incomplete without *ọ*; in the Bible, both were separated by a lexical space *ọ bụla* 'any'. If annotators had assigned *ọ* with a POS-tag 'PRN' (since it has pronoun form), identifying the right POS-tag for *bụla* became challenging since its meaning is incomplete. This was fixed by removing the lexical space between them. The main corpus size which was originally 264,795, after initial tokenization this was reduced to 263,854. Table 2 shows a few examples of tokens affected and solutions provided.

token id	token	error	resolved	total types
12291	ahụkwa	DEM/DEMXS	DEM_XS	138
4	nke	CJN/*	CJN	
26189	mkpịrịkpị	QTF/XXXX	NNQ	
59639	mpịakọta	NOTAG	NNC	156
1717	wit	XXXX	NNC	
58325	bụla	NOTAG	ọbụla/QTF	941
11790	ee	INT	INTJ	3827
815	chọọ	vSI_OVS	VSI_XS	
1073	fụọ	VSI_OVS	VSI_XS	
3537	nwee	OVS	VSI_XS	
7	banyere	VRV_XS	VrV_XS	

Table 2: Different error forms and corrections

4.2 Tagset Revision and Inter-Annotation Exercise

We used human annotators who are both Igbo linguists and native speakers for adding POS-tags to the Igbo text according to the initial tagset (TS0) guideline. There are factors that motivated the revision of TS0 in order to maximize human annotators agreement. The confusing factors we found among human annotators were related to the status of what to call participles, agentive/instrumental nouns, preposition, etc. For example, annotators had issue classifying some verbs when they change their structures as they precede or follow a pronoun. Mostly they chose to tag them participle (VPP) because the changed structure is prefixed *a/e*, which makes them look like participles. The worst case we found was the handling of the nominal class formed through verb nominalization with their inherent complements. There are agentive and instrumental nouns represented in POS-tag as NNAV NNAC and NNTV NNTC respectively, where V and C are the verbal and inherent noun components of the structure which should always appear as a linked pair. For example, *ọgụ/NNAV egwu/NNAC* "singer" and *ngwu/NNTV ji/NNTC* "digger", but link pairs like *ntachi obi* "steadfastness", *nnwere onwe* "freedom", etc are neither agentive nor instrumental nouns. These and many other issues led to evaluation and revision exercise of TS0. To solve the nominal class case, we redefined agentive and instrumental nouns into multi-word nouns (NNCV NNCC), so that all tokens in this class can easily fit in, which results as shown in table 5. We also introduced $alpha$_BPRN tags to clarify the difference between some verbs functions when prefixed with a vowel *a/e* caused by pronoun location on a sentence or caused by preceding auxiliary verbs. For instance, the word *esi* in *Ọ na- esi nri* "He is cooking " and *esi m Sheffield abịa* "I am coming from Sheffield" functions differently. The first is verb participle (VPP) because of the auxiliary verb *na-*, while the second is a simple verb inflected by a vowel prefix *e* as a result of the position of pronoun *m* in the sentence. Therefore, we introduced *VSI_BPRN* tag to indicate that *e* in *esi* is *m*-bound and *BPRN* tag for *m*-bound. It is assigned *VSI* if sentence pattern changes to *m si Sheffield abịa* "I am coming from Sheffield", while *m* is assign *PRN.*

The main objective we assigned to ourselves while revising the tagged corpus and tagset, was to get high quality tagged corpus and a specific tagset appropriate for Igbo and to maximize agreement among human annotators, in order to ensure high consistency of the tagged corpus. However, agreement among human annotators is not a guarantee for tagset quality, otherwise the trivial and uninformative tagset of one POS-tag size would be optimal. Most meaning-carrier words were assigned POS-tags based on the grammatical role they play in a sentence. Nevertheless, the more informative a tagset is, the less the taggers (human and automatic) accuracy tends to be. Therefore, one has to know where to strike a balance between the tagset informativeness and the tags performance. The tagset revision process affected its size because POS-tags were simplified, removed, and added: the size moved from 59 POS-tags to 62 POS-tags and finally to 69 POS-tags. The effects of some TS0 revisions are seen in the table 4.

4.2.1 Inter-Annotation Agreement

The Inter-annotation agreement process took three iterative phases, and four of the six annotators that produced ITC0 were used (two dropped out and another native speaker was employed instead). In each phase, a subset of main corpus was randomly selected. The tagging scheme used was evaluated and revised at each phase. Since there are 5 human annotators ($l1, l2, l3, l4, l5$, where l = linguist), each phase produced 5 annotations of the selected texts, and from these annotated texts we collate standard outputs through voting; for each token, we consider POS-tags with the highest agreement, while ignoring those with total disagreement. We take the collated outputs as our presumed truths, which serves as "silver standard" (SS) against which individual annotators are compared. The quality of the SS is determined by the annotators' tagging consistency calculated using inter-annotation agreement metrics as discussed in section 4.2.2. The SS and annotated texts ($tl1, tl2, tl3, tl4, tl5$) here will serve as TBL truth states in section 5.

	first IAA	second IAA	third IAA
# of sentences	150	150	150
# of tokens	4977	4963	4851

Table 3: IAA texts statistics

4.2.2 Measures

We adopted *Model and guidelines* $\rightarrow$ *Annotate* $\rightarrow$ *Evaluate* $\rightarrow$ *Revise* (M-A-E-R) methodology of (Pustejovsky and Stubbs, 2012), which is an internal part of MATTER annotation development cycle. We iteratively applied this *M-A-E-R* cycle, until all tags contributing huge disagreements in the annotations are corrected resulting in a higher consistency level among annotators. In each phase, the annotations *-A-* by annotators were done independently using our *M-* (model and guidelines). At the end of each phase, we collect all annotations and apply *-ER* (Evaluate and Revise). The whole process took 3 iterations of revision after cleaning and discussion before the final version. In each iteration, randomly selected texts from main corpus of size about 4.5k tokens was used, making a total of about 14k tokens on the whole (approximately 5% of the main corpus), see table 3. Performance was evaluated using f-measure, simple accuracy method and kappas. Our experiment assumed that each token is fully disambiguated, that is, one tag for one token *tok/t.*

In computing agreement, we use f-measure metric to provide a more detailed picture of inter-annotator agreement between annotators on individual parts-of-speech. The f-measure relates to precision and recall in the usual way. For each phase, we find the micro-average precision and recall, then calculate f-measure. In more detail, for the five annotators, given an annotator, *say* $l1$, we calculate its precision relative to silver standard (SS) developed (see section 4.2.1) with respect to a tag t in the set s of tags used, which is the number of tokens both SS and $l1$ agree to be t divided by the number of times SS say a token to be t *plus* number of times $l1$ has given t to a token different from both agreements. This is same calculation for recall only that division is by number of times $l1$ classify a token to be t *plus* number of times SS has given t to a token different from both agreements. See results in table 4.

Tag	Precision		
Tag	1st IAA	2nd IAA	3rd IAA
NNC	95.40	96.16	96.65
PRN	99.03	99.70	98.10
PREP	92.89	97.07	99.00
VPP	88.47	89.17	96.62
VSI	90.01	93.10	93.11
VIF_XS	88.96	68.43	95.49
VPERF	52.86	62.10	78.65
	Recall		
NNC	90.62	90.04	95.11
PRN	98.22	99.52	99.06
PREP	94.39	98.60	99.06
VPP	89.51	93.13	95.24
VSI	89.43	90.02	97.49
VIF_XS	58.46	84.38	85.00
VPERF	52.50	75.00	76.00
	f-measure		
NNC	92.31	92.45	95.36
PRN	98.12	99.11	98.07
PREP	93.09	97.32	98.53
VPP	88.04	90.13	95.33
VSI	88.39	90.90	94.71
VIF_XS	61.13	70.84	87.41
VPERF	45.05	59.36	71.59

Table 4: Some POS tags precision, recall and f-measure of first, second and third phases of annotations.

Tag	Precision		
	1st	2nd	3rd
NNAV	51.33	0.0	
NNAC	-	-	
NNTV	0.0	-	
NNTC	0.0	-	
	Recall		
NNAV	80.00	0.0	
NNAC	-	-	
NNTV	0.0	-	
NNTC	0.0	-	
	f-measure		
NNAV	55.52	0.0	
NNAC	-	-	
NNTV	0.0	-	
NNTC	0.0	-	
Solution			
Tag	Precision		
NNCV			77.81
NNCC			81.14
	Recall		
NNCV			73.33
NNCC			73.33
	f-measure		
NNCV			74.27
NNCC			75.79

Table 5: Some WORST POS tags precision, recall, and f-measure and solution proffered.

Also, we compute the overall agreement scores in two ways. Firstly, using the cohn's kappas and secondly, simple accuracy. We calculate

Accuracy = $\frac{tp}{N_n}$
where tp is true positive for all annotators and N_n is the total number of tokens of all classes combined together since they are same text.

kappas (k) = $\frac{A_o - A_e}{1 - A_e}$
where A_o is observed agreement, A_e is expected change agreement, A_o–A_e is how much agreement beyond chance was found and 1–A_e is how much agreement beyond chance is attainable (Raquel, 2011). So k is the proportion of the possible agreement beyond chance that was actually achieved. See results in table 6.

	Cohn Kappa			Raw agreement		
coders	1st	2nd	3rd	1st	2nd	3rd
l5+l2	81.35	85.49	91.28	83.14	86.78	92.08
l4+l3	91.77	89.23	92.65	92.51	90.17	93.28
l4+l5	83.96	84.57	88.55	85.39	85.92	89.55
l5+l3	83.76	86.08	90.91	85.19	87.27	91.71
l1+l3	84.56	89.60	95.49	86.00	90.53	95.84
l4+l1	86.36	90.09	91.98	87.62	90.99	92.62
l1+l2	84.80	98.71	92.84	86.32	98.83	93.44
l2+l3	85.97	89.27	92.91	87.30	90.23	93.57
l1+l5	84.88	85.17	89.66	86.28	86.50	90.52
l2+l4	86.82	89.44	90.59	88.11	90.41	91.45
Aves	**85.43**	**88.77**	**91.69**	**86.79**	**89.76**	**92.41**

Table 6: IAA scores based on Kappa statistics and simple accuracy formula for the first, second and third annotations.

5 TBL Propagation Method

We have created a satisfactory tagset (and associated guideline) through the revision of TS0. To create a gold standard of the Igbo corpus, which is what to use in training and testing machine learning classifiers, it is expected that those human annotators involved in the tagset revision cycle be used at this level as they have best understanding of the revised tagset to annotate the Igbo corpus afresh or to identify and correct changes on the initial tagged corpus based on the revised tagset, which will consume time and money. Instead we devised automatic method which used by-products of section 4.2.1 (annotated texts $(tl1, tl2, tl3, tl4, tl5)$) and output of section 4.1.1 (ITC1) to propagate changes found in the former to the latter, and flag locations where these changes occurred on ITC1 for inspection. Through this largely automated process, we expect to reduce the amount of human annotator time and effort, by only requiring the attention of a human annotator (the expert) on the marked positions instead of the entire text. Thus the quality of the corpus is increased with a minimum of expense. The approach of requiring that all revisions should be inspected by an expert annotator is needed to ensure a good quality end-product, with an accuracy that could not be achieved through a purely automated process.

There are two stages in this method, firstly, we used the silver standards (SS) developed from the collation of annotated texts $(tl1, tl2, tl3, tl4, tl5)$ (discussed in section 4.2.1) as the TBL truth state and "the corresponding subset" of ITC1 as TBL initial state. We trained a TBL learner on both states and applied these generated rules to the entire ITC1 to find errors on ITC1 and flag affected positions for inspections. The idea here is that the material from ITC1 is in erroneous state, as shown by its differences to the SS. TBL will learn rules to correct these errors. When the same rules are applied elsewhere in the corpus, the location where any rule 'fire' can be seen as candidate instances for of similar errors. All these locations are inspected by a human expert annotator. Since the TBL rule that fires at a location will propose a specific POS-tag change, the human expert can either accept the TBL proposed change, retain the existing tag at the location where the current POS-tag is deemed correct, or impose an alternative change according to his knowledge of revised tagset when neither TBL proposed tag or current tag are correct. For efficient inspections, we used the marked positions to get *word* current tag and contextual information, which helps in facilitating corrections.

1. Get silver standard from IAA to serve as TBL truth state, TS.
2. Take "the corresponding portion" of ITC1 to serve as TBL's initial state, IS.
3. Train TBL model on both TS and IS.
4. Apply TBL generated rules to ITC1.
5. Inspect locations where rules 'fire'.
6. Repeat from step 1 for TS from each phase of IAA.

# of iteration	TBL change accepted	no change	Manual change
1	3663	1215	420
2	1788	376	297
3	11161	3978	2592
	16612	**5569**	**3309**
Total inspected locations: 25,490			

Table 7: Result statistics after inspection

Table 7 gives detail of inspected flagged positions - the number of TBL changed tags accepted (where the current tag is not correct), rejected, where current tag prevailed, and neither TBL changed tag nor current tag was correct, so we chose from revised tagset. An improvement of 25,490 inspected locations were made on ITC1 with 19,921 effective changes giving ITC^I (improved ITC1).

Among the human annotators used in section 4.2.1, there are some that have better understanding of a particular POS-tag than the others. Therefore, some POS-tags that were voted out in silver standard creation might be correct if found and inspected, In this second stage, we went further to find in each of the annotated texts $(tl1, tl2, tl3, tl4, tl5)$ POS-tags that were not captured in the silver standard used in first stage. That is, finding and inspecting on ITC^I where one annotator's rule triggered and others did not and vice versa. In this experiment, instead of silver standard serving as TBL truth state, we used each of annotated texts $(tl1, tl2, tl3, tl4, tl5)$ and a subset of ITC^I as TBL initial state. The process steps are same with the first stage except line 6: *Repeat from step 1 for TS from annotated texts in each IAA phase*. In this stage, we find the impact of 1 annotated text by a human annotator ($l1$) weighted against 4 annotated texts of other four ($l2, l3, l4, l5$) on ITC^I. That is, for each TBL trained on both groups ($l1$ and $l2, l3, l4, l5$), we find and inspect word-tag pairs on ITC^I: where one annotator's rule fired and four others did not (grp1), where four annotators' rule fired and one did not (grp2), and where both fired (assigning the same POS-tag; grp3). In summary, out of 41,990 word-tag pairs flagged by this process, 39,151 is where grp1's rule fired, 2,468 where grp2's rule fired and 371 where grp3's rule fired. From these, 12,996 of 39,151, 1,836 of 2,468, and 318 of 371 have been inspected in the previous stage. All locations inspected by human expert are marked never to be inspected again because we believe that human expert judgement supersedes any other one. In whole, 26,839 word-tag pairs were inspected, out of which, effective change of 5,684 for grp1, 76 for grp2 and 6 for grp3 were made on ITC^I to give ITC2.

Note, in the both stages, TBL proposes additional changes, from which new rules can be formed in the next phase. Human annotators used in the tagset revision were not used beyond this point, except for the human expert who inspects the TBL changes on the original tagged corpus (ITC1). The corpus is automatically updated according to the accepted changes after the human expert's adjudication (table 11). The TBL model is retrained on the newly corrected corpus, and is thus updated after each iteration. The TBL deployed in this process is transformation-based learning on the fast-lane (fnTBL) by Ngai and Florian (2001), with the provided 40 rule templates at a threshold of 2. The output template for inspection is of the form P A B C, where P is the marked position (i), A is TBL changed tag (w_i/t^1), B is the current tag (w_i/t), and C is i's contextual information ($w_{i-2}/t \; w_{i-1}/t \; w_i/t \; w_{i+1}/t \; w_{i+2}/t$). See table 11 for sample results.

Finally, we performed manual error check on ITC2. Firstly, all tokens in ITC2 with POS-tags that are not in the revised tagset were checked and changed. This is done through building a tagset dictionary and passing ITC2 through it. Secondly, the TBL propagation process correctly reclassified some tokens in ITC1 with their new POS-tags introduced in the revised tagset. However, because of the small amount of corpus size used for TBL training, TBL lacked the capacity to apply learned rules widely on the ITC2 missing some instances that suppose to get the new POS-tags. To correct this, we used set of these new POS-tags to find tokens in ITC1 where they occurred, then we used these tokens to track all it's occurrences and their contexts for easy classification. This process corrected 4,994 *w/t* samples in ITC2 giving ITC3-current/first version of Igbo tagged corpus. Few examples of this process are shown in table 8. *ntachi obi* is an example of a multiword expression in Igbo meaning "steadfastness". They occur as a "link-pair" adjacent to each other without any intervening word. The second pair is complementing the meaning of the first. After TBL propagation method, as shown in ITC2 column, "ntachi" got a new POS-tag (NNCV) in 35 locations and it's pair "obi" also got NNCC in 35 locations. "obi" occurred 798 in entire text, it can occur on itself or adjacent to a verb or noun completing its meaning. We tracked all other locations in ITC2 where this link-pair occurred and inspect them to see whether they are suppose to get this tag or not. Outcome of our inspection is shown on the ITC3 column.

Token	Freq	ITC1	ITC2	ITC3
ntachi	38	NNC=35 VCO=1 NNAV=2	NNCV=35 NNC=1 NNAV=2	NNCV=38
obi	38	NNC=37 PRN = 1	NNCC=35 NNC=2 PRN=1	NNCC=38
ntụkwasị	67	VSI_XS=5 NNAV=1 VCO=6 NNC=55	NNCV=26 NNC=40 NNAV=1	NNCV=67
obi	67	NNC=67	NNCC=27 NNC=40	NNCC=67

Table 8: Some examples of manual error check and corrections

6 Evaluations

We present evaluation results for all the outputs of the above process: ITC0, ITC1, ITC2 and ITC3 to show improvement rates. For the evaluation performance, we split the corpora into 10 folds. 10-fold subsets were created by slicing the the corpora into 822 sentences, each is 25,981 words on the average. Slicing on the sentences is making sure that each piece contained full sentences (rather than cutting off the text in the middle of a sentence). For 10-fold steps and on closed vocabulary, we trained TBL classifier on 9-fold and tested on the held-out. The results are summarised in table 9.

Fold	Accuracy			
	ITC0	ITC1	ITC2	ITC3
0	84.509	88.748	94.027	94.462
1	90.522	91.413	93.171	93.653
2	90.743	90.809	92.871	93.682
3	92.153	92.474	94.214	94.489
4	92.098	93.119	94.687	94.816
5	81.980	85.974	93.151	93.492
6	89.342	90.589	93.215	93.809
7	85.684	88.433	93.287	93.691
8	88.186	89.913	93.621	94.063
9	86.996	90.190	93.409	93.920
Average	**88.221**	**90.166**	**93.565**	**94.007**

Table 9: Simple accuracy on 10-fold evaluation

7 Discussion and Re-usability

We trained TBL classifiers on the inter-annotation agreement (IAA) annotated texts ($tl1, tl2, tl3, tl4, tl5$) with the assumption that errors flagged with the rule-based model generated will be the type of errors that occur in these texts. If we presume that these errors are evenly distributed, then we can assume that the most common types of errors will also occur frequently in the annotated texts, and are likely to be flagged in the full text. The effect of this assumption explored in section 5 is seen in table 10. A few samples from this experiment are displayed in table 11. The columns show the affected samples, TBL suggested tags, accepted (whether the TBL suggested tag was accepted by the human expert), manual correction (if TBL suggested tag and current ITC1 tag were wrong), and final state of tags. Interestingly, some tokens were correctly reclassified, even new tags introduced in the IAA exercises as a result of the tagset revision are correctly inserted into the main text. The Igbo corpus size of 263,854 tokens, which initially had 54 tags annotated according to the tagset reported in Onyenwe et al., (2014), now contains 66 tags, including all changes in the revised tagset.

We performed evaluation on the outputs from all of the process starting from the initial state of the main text to the improved state (ITC0 to ITC3) in section 6. From the table 9, we can deduce that there is constant improvement on the pattern consistency in the tagged corpus after each process. A total improvement score of 5.79% was achieved; manual cleaning gave 1.95% improvement, TBL propagation gave an additional 3.40%,

Token	Frequency of word in Maintxt	Frequency of word affected by the process
n'	11570	164
ndị	5755	3688
unu	3816	1389
a	3696	1350
onwe	831	828
banyere	611	503
olee	159	53
keenụ	3	1

Table 10: Frequency of words found in main text and TBL flagged samples

and manual check up another 0.44%. Improvement processes flagged 62,385 word–tag pair positions which were inspected by an expert human annotator, contributed 23.93% improvement on the tagged Igbo corpus.

The Igbo language has 30 dialects as a result of nasality and aspiration[5]. Our tagset and corpus annotation is based on the standard Igbo, which omits the nasality and aspiration found in those dialects. The tagset and associated guideline are applicable to all 30 dialects, since these dialectal words play the same grammatical role as found in the standard Igbo texts, through which the tagset was developed. For example, the interrogative sentence *olee aha gị?* "what is your name?" in standard Igbo is said in different dialects as *ndee afụa gụ?*, *ndee awa ghụ?*, etc. "ndee" is equivalent to "olee" which makes the sentence interrogative, *afụa, ewa* is equal to "aha" and *gụ, ghụ* is equal to "gị". Therefore, if we create a dictionary of word-types from the Bible in all dialects, with standard Igbo as a reference point, the annotated Bible corpus in standard Igbo can be used to annotate other dialects with minimal errors.

8 Conclusion and Further Work

We have presented a methodology to propagate POS-tag changes made during an inter-annotation agreement exercise due to tagset revisions on the main corpus. Our semi-automatic method, shows that even the new tags introduced in the IAA were found, and wrongly tagged tokens on ITC0 that were corrected in the IAA exercise were identified in the refined Igbo tagged corpus (ITC3). This is because the errors that TBL flagged are the types of errors that occur in the inter-annotation text. Through this process, we improved the quality of original Igbo tagged corpus by reflecting

[5] http://www.ethnogue.com/language/ibo [August, 2015]

Instance	TBL POS-tag	Accepted	Manual Change	Final POS-Tag	Meaning
ahụ/DEM	VPP	YES		VPP	see
ahụ/DEM	VPP	NO		DEM	that
n'/VAX	PREP	YES		PREP	in/on/from
na/VAX	CJN	YES		CJN	and
na-/NNC	VAX	YES		YES	auxiliary verb (AV)
onye/NNM	NNC	YES		YES	person
ndị/NNC	NNM	YES		YES	people of
onwe/PRNREF	PRNEMP	YES		PRNEMP	self
ya/PRN	PRNREF	NO		PRN	her/him
unu/NNM	PRN	YES		PRN	plural you
dịkwa/VCO	VSI_XS	YES		VSI_XS	is also
kọrọ/VrV	VPP_XS	NO		VrV	told
nyere/VCO	VSI_XS	NO	VrV	VrV	gave
ná/CJN	PREP	YES		PREP	in/on/from
a/DEM	PRN	NO		DEM	this
a/DEM	PRN	YES		PRN	impersonal pronoun (IP)
ana/VPP	VAX_BPRN	YES		VAX_BPRN	AV "na" with pronoun prefix "a"
m/PRN	BPRN	YES		BPRN	"I" bound to "a/e" pronoun
óké/NNC	NNH	YES		NNH	boundary
nwere/VrV	VMOV	YES		VMOV	[nwere ike] can
ike/NNC	VMOC	YES		VMOC	[nwere ike] can
ekwesị/VPP_XS	VPP	NO	BCN	BCN	right/correct
ònye/WH	NNC	NO		WH	who
ntachi/NNC	NNCV	YES		NNCV	[ntachi obi] steadfastness
obi/NNC	NNCC	YES		NNCC	[ntachi obi] steadfastness
esi/VPP	VSI_BPRN_XS	NO	VSI_BPRN	VSI_BPRN	simple verb "si" with pronoun prefix "e'

Table 11: Some samples of flagged locations inspected.

changes from the tagset revision made in the inter-annotation agreement exercise on it. We also applied TBL on each annotated text of the inter-annotation agreement exercise. These different rule sets generated can be used to identify locations for inspection across the whole corpus, for example, where the rules for most annotators suggest a tag where another annotator disagree. This finds and inspect where one annotator disagrees with majority, because among annotators, some are have better insight than others on a particular tag. Further more, manual error check was used to find and correct instances our propagation method affected but could not fire in all locations where they occurred. The evaluation result shows that we achieved an improvement of 5.786% over the entire process. The effort, time and money that would had been used to manually execute this were saved. In total, the entire processes gave 62,385 (23.92% of main corpus) positions inspected on the main corpus with 35,743 effective changes made.

The TBL propagation method used here can generalize to many annotation problems, especially low-resource languages since TBL has been classified to work well not only on large sized corpus but also on small amount of corpus. In Africa, of around 2000 languages in the continent, only a small number have featured in the NLP research field. This work is a good direction for them to co-opt our technique in POS-tagging their texts, which is a primary step in developing NLP resource tools.

The text of this annotated corpus is in standard Igbo. It is potentially re-usable on other dialects or genres towards developing annotated corpora with correctable errors. The only foreseen challenge in moving from religious genre used in this paper to other genres or from standard dialect to other dialects is the problem of unknown words, which is mainly caused by agglutinative nature of the language. We plan to further this research by developing the first Igbo POS-tagger, deal with handling of unknown words and develop annotated corpora for other dialects through the already tagged corpus. This work, to the best of our knowledge, developed the first tagged corpus for Igbo which is geared towards supporting computational NLP research on the language.

Acknowledgments

We acknowledge the financial support of Tertiary Education Trust Fund (TETFund), Nigeria and Nnamdi Azikiwe University, Awka, Nigeria.

References

Ron Artstein and Poesio Massimo. 2008. *Inter-coder agreement for computational linguistics.* MIT Press, (34)4:555–596.

Eric Brill. 1992. *A Simple Rule-based Part of Speech Tagger.* Proceedings of the Third Conference on Applied Natural Language Processing, ANLC '92. Association for Computational Linguistics, Stroudsburg, PA, USA.

Nọlue E. Emenanjo. 1999. *Elements of Modern Igbo Grammar: A Descriptive Approach.* Ibadan Oxford University Press.

Annette M. Green. 1997. *Kappa Statistics for Multiple Raters Using Categorical Classifications* Proceedings of the Twenty-Second Annual SAS Users Group International Conference, San, Diego, CA.

Sigrún Helgadóttir and Hrafn Loftsson and Eiríkur Rgnvaldsson. 2012. *Correcting Errors in a New Gold Standard for Tagging Icelandic Text.* LREC'14: 2944-2948.

Clara Ikekeonwu. 1999. *Igbo", Handbook of the International Phonetic Association.* Cambridge University Press.

Klaus Krippendorff. 1980. *Content Analysis: An Introduction to Its Methodology* Sage, Beverly Hills, CA.

Richard J. Landis and Gary G. Koch. 1977. *The measurement of observer agreement for categorical data* biometrics, 159–174, JSTOR.

Hrafn Loftsson 2009. *Correcting a POS-Tagged Corpus Using Three Complementary Methods* In Proceedings of EACL-09, 523–531.

Grace Ngai and Radu Florian. 2001. *Transformation-based learning in the fast lane.* In Proceedings of North Americal ACL.

Ikechukwu E. Onyenwe and Chinedu Uchechukwu and Mark Hepple. 2014. *Part-of-speech Tagset and Corpus Development for Igbo, an African.* LAW VIII, 2014.

James Pustejovsky and Amber Stubbs. 2012. *Natural Language Annotation for Machine Learning.* O'Reilly Media, Inc.

Fernández Raquel. 2011. *Assessing the Reliability of an Annotation Scheme for Indefinites Measuring Inter–annotator Agreement* Institute for Logic, Language and Computation University of Amsterdam.

Chinedu Uchechukwu. 2008. *African Language Data Processing: The Example of the Igbo Language.* 10th International pragmatics conference, Data processing in African languages.

WikiTrans: Swedish-Danish Machine Translation in a Constraint Grammar Framework (invited talk)

Eckhard Bick
Institute of Language and Communication
University of Southern Denmark
eckhard.bick@mail.dk

1 Abstract

This talk presents an MT system for the automatic generation of Danish Wikipedia articles from Swedish originals. The translated Wikipedia (WikiTrans) is indexed for both title and content, and integrated with original Danish articles where they exist. Newly added or modified articles in the Swedish Wikipedia are monitored and handled on a daily basis. The translation approach (GramTrans) uses a grammar-based machine translation system with a deep, structural source-language analysis. Morphosyntactic disambiguation and lexical transfer rules exploit Constraint Grammar tags and dependency links to access contextual information, such as syntactic argument function, semantic type and quantifiers. Out-of-vocabulary words are handled by derivational and compound analysis with a combined coverage of 99.3%, as well as systematic morpho-phonemic transliterations for the remaining cases. Reflecting the similarities between Swedish and Danish, the system achieved high BLEU scores (0.65-0.8 depending on references), and outperformed standard STMT and RBMT competitors by a large margin.

2 Biography

Dr. Eckhard Bick is a computational linguist and project leader for the VISL lab at the University of Southern Denmark, where he works as a language technology researcher at the Department of Language and Communication (ISK). Over the years he has designed and developed grammars, corpora, lexical resources and applicational tools for a large number of languages, including most of the Romance and Germanic languages. Eckhard Bick is a leading expert in the field of Constraint Grammar, with a current focus on semantic annotation and machine translation. Eckhard Bick has published extensively on various aspects of computational linguistics and participated in a large number of international research projects.

Proceedings of the Joint Workshop on Language Technology for Closely Related Languages, Varieties and Dialects, page 34,
Hissar, Bulgaria, September 10, 2015.

Language Identification using Classifier Ensembles

Shervin Malmasi
Centre for Language Technology
Macquarie University
Sydney, NSW, Australia
shervin.malmasi@mq.edu.au

Mark Dras
Centre for Language Technology
Macquarie University
Sydney, NSW, Australia
mark.dras@mq.edu.au

Abstract

In this paper we describe the language identification system we developed for the Discriminating Similar Languages (DSL) 2015 shared task. We constructed a classifier ensemble composed of several Support Vector Machine (SVM) base classifiers, each trained on a single feature type. Our feature types include character 1–6 grams and word unigrams and bigrams. Using this system we were able to outperform the other entries in the closed training track of the DSL 2015 shared task, achieving the best accuracy of 95.54%.

1 Introduction

Language Identification (LID) is the task of determining the language of a given text, which may be at the document, sub-document or even sentence level. Although the task is generally considered to be a solved problem, recently attention has turned to discriminating between close languages or variants. This includes pairings such as Malay-Indonesian and Croatian-Serbian (Ljubesic et al., 2007), or even varieties of one language (British *vs.* American English).

This has motivated the organization of the Discriminating Similar Languages (DSL) 2015 shared task where the aim is to build systems for distinguishing such pairs. The 2015 edition included 14 language classes.

LID has a number of useful applications including lexicography, authorship profiling, machine translation and Information Retrieval. Another example is the application of the output from these LID methods to adapt NLP tools that require annotated data, such as part-of-speech taggers, for resource-poor languages.

2 Related Work

Work in LID dates back to the seminal research of Beesley (1988), Cavnar and Trenkle (1994) and Dunning (1994). Automatic LID methods have since been widely used in NLP. Although LID can be extremely accurate in distinguishing languages that use distinct character sets (e.g. Chinese or Japanese) or are very dissimilar (e.g. Spanish and Swedish), performance is degraded when it is used for discriminating similar languages or dialects. This has led to researchers turning their attention to the sub-problem of discriminating between closely-related languages and varieties.

This issue has been researched in the context of confusable languages, including Malay-Indonesian (Bali, 2006), Farsi-Dari (Malmasi and Dras, 2015a), Croatian-Slovene-Serbian (Ljubesic et al., 2007), Portuguese varieties (Zampieri and Gebre, 2012), Spanish varieties (Zampieri et al., 2013), and Chinese varieties (Huang and Lee, 2008). The task of Arabic Dialect Identification has also drawn attention in the Arabic NLP community (Malmasi et al., 2015a).

This issue was also the focus of the first "Discriminating Similar Language" (DSL) shared task[1] in 2014. The shared task used data from 13 different languages and varieties divided into 6 sub-groups and teams needed to build systems for distinguishing these classes. They were provided with a training and development dataset comprised of 20,000 sentences from each language and an unlabelled test set of 1,000 sentences per language was used for evaluation. Most entries used surface features and many applied hierarchical classifiers, taking advantage of the structure provided by the language family memberships of the 13 classes. More details can be found in the shared task report by Zampieri et al. (2014).

[1]This was part of the Workshop on Applying NLP Tools to Similar Languages, Varieties and Dialects, which was co-located with COLING 2014

Proceedings of the Joint Workshop on Language Technology for Closely Related Languages, Varieties and Dialects, pages 35–43,
Hissar, Bulgaria, September 10, 2015. ©2015 Association for Computational Linguistics

Language	Code	Train	Dev	Test
Bulgarian	BG	18,000	2,000	1,000
Bosnian	BS	18,000	2,000	1,000
Czech	CZ	18,000	2,000	1,000
Spanish (Argentina)	ES_AR	18,000	2,000	1,000
Spanish (Spain)	ES_ES	18,000	2,000	1,000
Croatian	HR	18,000	2,000	1,000
Indonesian	ID	18,000	2,000	1,000
Malaysian	MY	18,000	2,000	1,000
Macedonian	MK	18,000	2,000	1,000
Portuguese (Brazil)	PT_BR	18,000	2,000	1,000
Portuguese (Portugal)	PT_PT	18,000	2,000	1,000
Slovak	SK	18,000	2,000	1,000
Serbian	SR	18,000	2,000	1,000
Other	XX	18,000	2,000	1,000
Total		252,000	28,000	14,000

Table 1: The languages included in the corpus and the number of sentences in each set.

3 Data

The data for the shared task comes from the DSL Corpus Collection (Tan et al., 2014). The task is performed at the sentence-level and the corpus consists of 294,000 sentences distributed evenly between 14 language classes. The corpus is subdivided into training, development and test sets. The languages and the number of sentences in each set are listed in Table 1.

An interesting addition to this year's data is the inclusion of an "other" class which contains data from various additional languages. The motivation here is to emulate a realistic language identification and see how the systems perform in classifying previously unseen languages.

More details about the data can be found in the shared task overview paper (Zampieri et al., 2015).

4 Method

In this section we describe the general methodology used to construct our system. We use a supervised learning approach based on discriminative classifiers.

4.1 Features

We use two basic classes of surface features: character n-grams (n = 1–6) and word n-grams (n = 1–2).

4.2 Classifier

We use a linear Support Vector Machine to perform multi-class classification in our experiments. In particular, we use the LIBLINEAR[2] package (Fan et al., 2008) which has been shown to be efficient for text classification problems such as this. For example, it has been demonstrated to be a very effective classifier for the task of Native Language Identification (Malmasi and Dras, 2015b; Malmasi et al., 2013) which also relies on text classification methods.

5 Classifier Ensembles

Classifier ensembles are a way of combining different classifiers or experts with the goal of improving accuracy through enhanced decision making. They have been applied to a wide range of real-world problems and shown to achieve better results compared to single-classifier methods (Oza and Tumer, 2008). Through aggregating the outputs of multiple classifiers in some way, their outputs are generally considered to be more robust. Ensemble methods continue to receive increasing attention from researchers and remain a focus of much machine learning research (Woźniak et al., 2014; Kuncheva and Rodríguez, 2014).

Such ensemble-based systems often use a parallel architecture, as illustrated in Figure 1, where the classifiers are run independently and their outputs are aggregated using a fusion method. Other, more sophisticated, ensemble methods that rely on meta-learning may employ a stacked architecture where the output from a first set of classifiers is fed into a second level meta-classifier and so on.

[2] http://www.csie.ntu.edu.tw/%7Ecjlin/liblinear/

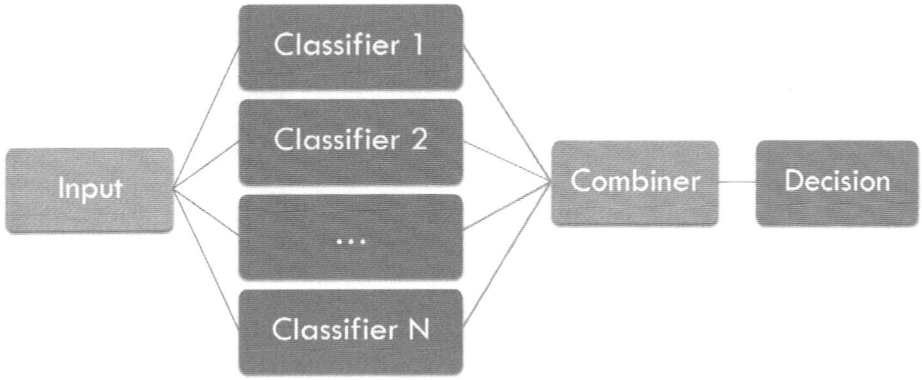

Figure 1: An example of parallel classifier ensemble architecture where N independent classifiers provide predictions which are then fused using an ensemble combination method.

The first part of creating an ensemble is generating the individual classifiers. Various methods for creating these ensemble elements have been proposed. These involve using different algorithms, parameters or feature types; applying different preprocessing or feature scaling methods and varying (*e.g.* distorting or resampling) the training data.

For example, *Bagging* (bootstrap aggregating) is a commonly used method for ensemble generation (Breiman, 1996) that can create multiple base classifiers. It works by creating multiple bootstrap training sets from the original training data and a separate classifier is trained from each one of these sets. The generated classifiers are said to be diverse because each training set is created by sampling with replacement and contains a random subset of the original data. *Boosting* (*e.g.* with the AdaBoost algorithm) is another method where the base models are created with different weight distributions over the training data with the aim of assigning higher weights to training instances that are misclassified (Freund and Schapire, 1996).

As we describe in section 7, each of the base classifiers in our ensemble is trained on a different feature space, as this has proven to be effective.

The second part of ensemble design is choosing a fusion rule to aggregate the outputs from the various learners, this is discussed in the next section.

6 Ensemble Combination Methods

Once it has been decided how the set of base classifiers will be generated, selecting the classifier combination method is the next fundamental design question in ensemble construction.

The answer to this question depends on what output is available from the individual classifiers. Some combination methods are designed to work with class labels, assuming that each learner outputs a single class label prediction for each data point. Other methods are designed to work with class-based continuous output, requiring that for each instance every classifier provides a measure of confidence probability[3] for each class label. These outputs for each class usually sum to 1 over all the classes.

Although a number of different fusion methods have been proposed and tested, there is no single dominant method (Polikar, 2006). The performance of these methods is influenced by the nature of the problem and available training data, the size of the ensemble, the base classifiers used and the diversity between their outputs.

The selection of this method is often done empirically. Many researchers have compared and contrasted the performance of combiners on different problems, and most of these studies – both empirical and theoretical – do not reach a definitive conclusion (Kuncheva, 2014, p 178).

In the same spirit, we experiment with several information fusion methods which have been widely discussed in the machine learning literature. Our selected methods are listed below. Various other methods exist and the interested reader can refer to the exposition by Polikar (2006).

[3] *i.e.* an estimate of the posterior probability for the label. For non-probabilistic classifiers the distance to the decision boundary is used for estimating the decision likelihoods.

6.1 Plurality voting

Each classifier votes for a single class label. The votes are tallied and the label with the highest number[4] of votes wins. Ties are broken arbitrarily. This voting method is very simple and does not have any parameters to tune. An extensive analysis of this method and its theoretical underpinnings can be found in the work of (Kuncheva, 2004, p. 112).

6.2 Mean Probability Rule

The probability estimates for each class are added together and the class label with the highest average probability is the winner. This is equivalent to the probability sum combiner which does not require calculating the average for each class. An important aspect of using probability outputs in this way is that a classifier's support for the true class label is taken in to account, even when it is not the predicted label (*e.g.* it could have the second highest probability). This method has been shown to work well on a wide range of problems and, in general, it is considered to be simple, intuitive, stable (Kuncheva, 2014, p. 155) and resilient to estimation errors (Kittler et al., 1998) making it one of the most robust combiners discussed in the literature.

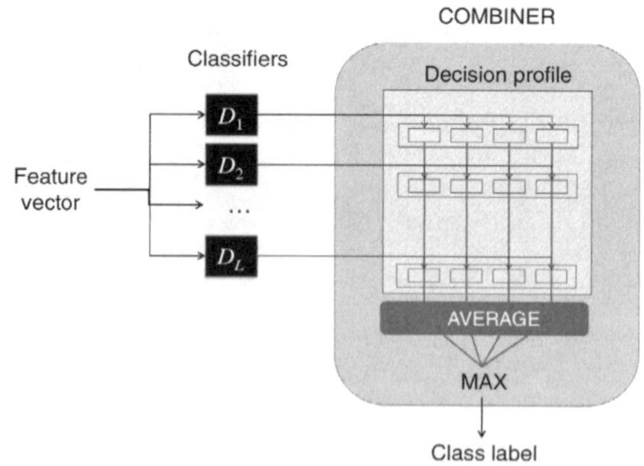

Figure 2: An example of a mean probability combiner. The feature vector for a sample is input to L different classifiers, each of which output a vector of confidence probabilities for each possible class label. These vectors are combined to form the decision profile for the instance which is used to calculate the average support given to each label. The label with the maximum support is then chosen as the prediction. Image reproduced from (Kuncheva, 2014).

6.3 Median Probability Rule

Given that the mean probability used in the above rule is sensitive to outliers, an alternative is to use the median as a more robust estimate of the mean (Kittler et al., 1998). Under this rule each class label's estimates are sorted and the median value is selected as the final score for that label. The label with the highest median value is picked as the winner. As with the mean combiner, this method measures the central tendency of support for each label as a means of reaching a consensus decision.

6.4 Product Rule

For each class label, all of the probability estimates are multiplied together to create the label's final estimate (Polikar, 2006, p. 37). The label with the highest estimate is selected. This rule can provide the best overall estimate of posterior probability for a label, given that the individual estimates are accurate. A trade-off here is that this method is very sensitive to low probabilities: a single low score for a label from any classifier will essentially eliminate that class label.

6.5 Highest Confidence

In this simple method, the class label that receives the vote with the largest degree of confidence is selected as the final prediction (Kuncheva, 2014, p. 150). In contrast to the previous methods, this combiner disregards the consensus opinion and instead picks the prediction of the expert with the highest degree of confidence.

6.6 Borda Count

This method works by using each classifier's confidence estimates to create a ranked list of the class labels in order of preference, with the predicted label at rank 1. The winning label is then selected using the Borda count[5] algorithm (Ho et al., 1994). The algorithm works by assigning points to labels based on their ranks. If there are N different labels, then each classifiers' preferences are assigned points as follows: the top-ranked label receives N points, the second place label receives

[4]This differs with a *majority* voting combiner where a label must obtain over 50% of the votes to win. However, the names are sometimes used interchangeably.

[5]This method is generally attributed to Jean-Charles de Borda (1733–1799), but evidence suggests that it was also proposed by Ramon Llull (1232–1315).

$N - 1$ points, third place receives $N - 2$ points and so on with the last preference receiving a single point. These points are then tallied to select the winner with the highest score.

The most obvious advantage of this method is that it takes into account each classifier's preferences, making it possible for a label to win even if another label received the majority of the first preference votes.

6.7 Oracle

We use an "Oracle" combiner as one possible approach to estimating the upper-bound for classification accuracy. This method has previously been used to analyze the limits of majority vote classifier combination (Kuncheva et al., 2001). The oracle will assign the correct class label for an instance if at least one of the constituent classifiers in the ensemble produces the correct label for that data point. Oracles are usually used in comparative experiments and to gauge the performance and diversity of the classifiers chosen for an ensemble (Kuncheva, 2002; Kuncheva et al., 2003). They can help us quantify the *potential* upper limit of an ensemble's performance on the given data and how this performance varies with different ensemble configurations (Malmasi et al., 2015b).

7 Systems

We test three different systems in our submissions to the shared task, as outlined here.

7.1 System 1

We train a single model based on a simple combination of all our feature types into a single feature space. The model has approximately 13.6 million features. This was the first system that we built and it achieved very good results of 94-95% during testing. It was selected as our first submission.

7.2 System 2

The second system is an ensemble classifier, as described in section 5. The aim here was to improve over the single classifier system described in section 7.1. Each base classifier in the ensemble is trained on a separate feature type, resulting in a total of eight classifiers in the system.

During the development of our system we tested the six ensemble fusion methods described in section 6. Our experiments with the training and development data showed that the mean probability combiner yielded the best accuracy.

We achieved an accuracy of 95.5% on the development set against an oracle accuracy of 99%, showing that the combiner was very close to the upper-bound of possible classification accuracy. This result was slightly better than that of System 1, so this method was selected for our second submission. The results from the other combiners were also in a similar range, but we used the mean probability combiner for our second system.

7.3 System 3

Our final system is identical to the second system in its method and setup with the exception that some weak and redundant features were removed. We suspected that there may be some redundancy in the large number of character n-gram features and removing these might increase the diversity, and thus accuracy, of the ensemble.

Using the feature analysis methodology outlined by Malmasi and Cahill (2015), we analyzed the feature interactions using the training and development sets. This methodology uses Yule's Q-coefficient statistic (Yule, 1912), which can be a useful measure of pairwise dependence between two classifiers (Kuncheva et al., 2003). This notion of dependence relates to complementarity and orthogonality, and is an important factor in combining classifiers (Lam, 2000). The calculated Q-coefficient ranges between -1 to $+1$, where -1 signifies negative association, 0 indicates no association (independence) and $+1$ means perfect positive correlation (dependence). We apply this method to our ensemble to calculate the dependence between the classifiers. The results for the analysis are shown as a heat map in Figure 3.

We see that the predictions obtained using character unigrams are very diverse to the other features, as noted by the low Q-coefficient. This diversity is a result of character unigrams being a weak feature: they only achieve around 76% accuracy whereas most other feature types can obtain $> 90\%$ accuracy. As a result we removed this feature from the ensemble.

Character bigrams are diverse and also have a higher accuracy, so they were retained. Character trigrams are very similar to 4-grams and their accuracies are close, so we remove the trigrams. The same applies to character 5- and 6-grams, and we decided to remove the 5-grams. Character 4-grams were retained since they had good accuracy and diversity, *e.g.* with word bigrams.

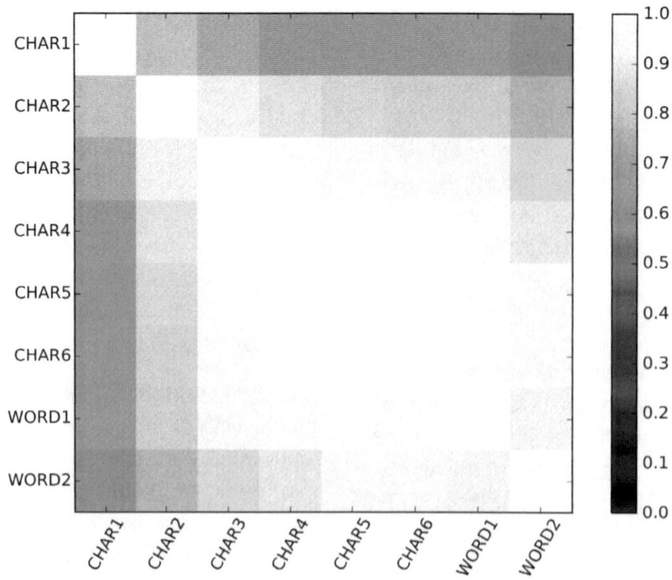

Figure 3: The matrix of pairwise Q-coefficient values between our feature types, displayed as a heat map. Smaller values indicate lower dependence between their predictions.

	Normal		NE Removed	
	Rank	**Accuracy**	**Rank**	**Accuracy**
Random Baseline	—	7.14%	—	7.14%
System 1	3	95.31%	2	93.88%
System 2	2	95.44%	3	93.73%
System 3	**1**	**95.54%**	**1**	**94.01%**

Table 2: Results for our three system on the test set. The accuracy and rank among all systems in the shared task are shown. Our optimized ensemble ranked first in both tasks.

To recap, our third system is a modification of the second system where we remove character 1-, 3- and 5-grams in order to increase the ensemble diversity. This reduced ensemble was chosen as our third submission as it achieved slightly higher results than the full ensemble during development.

8 Results

We entered our systems in both sub-tasks of the closed training track. We did not enter the open training track of the competition. The first subtask (the "normal" task) required our system to classify 14,000 unlabelled sentences. The second task was also similar, but it used a different set of sentences which also had all named entities (NE) removed ("NE Removed" task). This is because it is assumed that features related to NEs can strongly influence the results.

Our systems took the top three places for both subtasks. The results and rankings for each system are shown in Table 2. We note that System 3 — the optimized ensemble — was the winning entry for both tasks. This comports with our initial tests where it was our best system during development.

The confusion matrix for our best results in the normal task are shown in Figure 4. We achieved a perfect 100% accuracy for four classes: Czech (`CZ`), Macedonian (`MK`), Slovak (`SK`) and Other (`XX`). Bulgarian (`BG`) was also close with only a single sentence being misclassified as Macedonian. These results suggest that confusion between Bulgarian–Macedonian and Czech–Slovak is not a significant issue here. The greatest confusion is between the Bosnian–Croatian–Serbian[6] group as well as the Spanish and Portuguese dialect pairs. Bosnian is the worst performing language among the 14 classes.

We also analyze the learning rate for the features in our system. The cross-validation accuracy for four different feature types is shown in Figure 5. Higher order character n-grams seem to outperform word n-grams. Word bigrams are lower in accuracy and have a steeper learning rate.

[6]We also observe that Bosnian is the most confused class among the three while Serbian has the least errors.

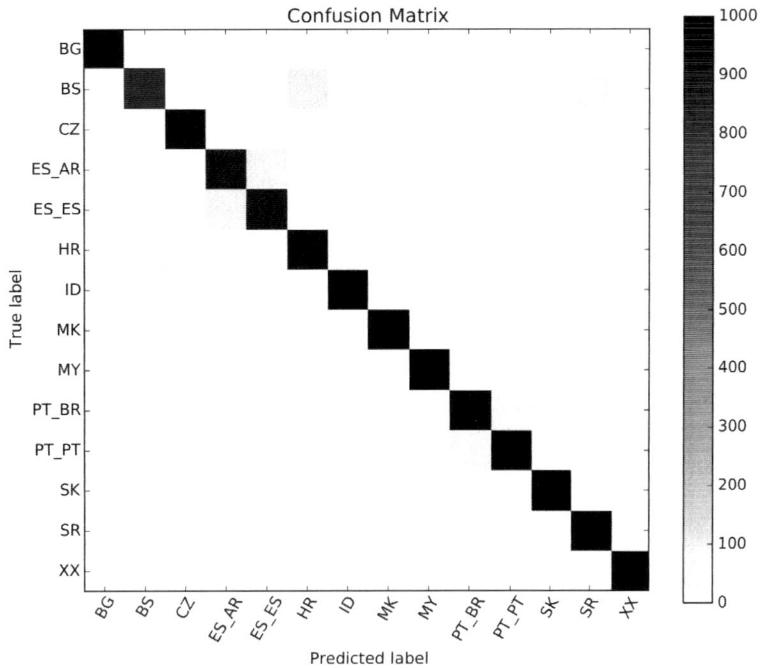

Figure 4: The confusion matrix for our results on the test set (normal task).

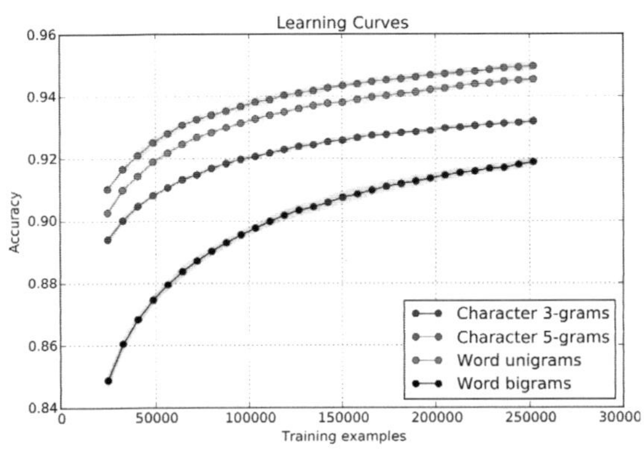

Figure 5: Learning curves for some of our features based on cross-validation accuracy. We observe that character n-grams perform better than word-based n-grams. The accuracy does not plateau with the entire training data used.

We also observe that accuracy increases continuously as the training data is increased. This suggests that despite the already large size of the training set, there is still room for further improvement by adding more data. However, this would also result in an increase in the size of our feature space, which is already quite large due to the prodigious growth rate of the larger order character n-grams.

9 Discussion and Conclusion

In this work we demonstrated the utility of classifier ensembles for text classification. Using an ensemble composed of base classifiers trained on character 1–6 grams and word unigrams and bigrams, we were able to outperform the other entries in the closed track of the DSL 2015 shared task.

A crucial direction for future work is the investigation of methods to reduce the confusion between these three groups of classes.

In this work we did not experiment with feature selection methods to evaluate if this can further enhance performance, or at least efficiency by reducing the dimensionality of the feature space. One weakness of our system may be the very high dimensionality of the feature space with almost 14 million features. Having such a large number of features can be inefficient and may impede the use of our system for real-time applications.

References

Ranaivo-Malançon Bali. 2006. Automatic Identification of Close Languages–Case Study: Malay and Indonesian. *ECTI Transaction on Computer and Information Technology*, 2(2):126–133.

Kenneth R Beesley. 1988. Language identifier: A computer program for automatic natural-language identification of on-line text. In *Proceedings of the 29th Annual Conference of the American Translators Association*, volume 47, page 54. Citeseer.

Leo Breiman. 1996. Bagging predictors. In *Machine Learning*, pages 123–140.

William B. Cavnar and John M. Trenkle. 1994. N-Gram-Based Text Categorization. In *Proceedings of SDAIR-94, 3rd Annual Symposium on Document Analysis and Information Retrieval*, pages 161–175, Las Vegas, US.

Ted Dunning. 1994. *Statistical identification of language*. Computing Research Laboratory, New Mexico State University.

Rong-En Fan, Kai-Wei Chang, Cho-Jui Hsieh, Xiang-Rui Wang, and Chih-Jen Lin. 2008. LIBLINEAR: A Library for Large Linear Classification. *Journal of Machine Learning Research*, 9:1871–1874.

Yoav Freund and Robert E Schapire. 1996. Experiments with a new boosting algorithm. In *ICML*, volume 96, pages 148–156.

Tin Kam Ho, Jonathan J. Hull, and Sargur N. Srihari. 1994. Decision combination in multiple classifier systems. *Pattern Analysis and Machine Intelligence, IEEE Transactions on*, 16(1):66–75.

Chu-Ren Huang and Lung-Hao Lee. 2008. Contrastive Approach towards Text Source Classification based on Top-Bag-Word Similarity.

Josef Kittler, Mohamad Hatef, Robert PW Duin, and Jiri Matas. 1998. On combining classifiers. *IEEE Transactions on Pattern Analysis and Machine Intelligence*, 20(3):226–239.

Ludmila I Kuncheva and Juan J Rodríguez. 2014. A weighted voting framework for classifiers ensembles. *Knowledge and Information Systems*, 38(2):259–275.

Ludmila I Kuncheva, James C Bezdek, and Robert PW Duin. 2001. Decision templates for multiple classifier fusion: an experimental comparison. *Pattern Recognition*, 34(2):299–314.

Ludmila I Kuncheva, Christopher J Whitaker, Catherine A Shipp, and Robert PW Duin. 2003. Limits on the majority vote accuracy in classifier fusion. *Pattern Analysis & Applications*, 6(1):22–31.

Ludmila I Kuncheva. 2002. A theoretical study on six classifier fusion strategies. *IEEE Transactions on pattern analysis and machine intelligence*, 24(2):281–286.

Ludmila I Kuncheva. 2004. *Combining Pattern Classifiers: Methods and Algorithms*. John Wiley & Sons.

Ludmila I Kuncheva. 2014. *Combining Pattern Classifiers: Methods and Algorithms*. Wiley, second edition.

Louisa Lam. 2000. Classifier combinations: implementations and theoretical issues. In *Multiple classifier systems*, pages 77–86. Springer.

Nikola Ljubesic, Nives Mikelic, and Damir Boras. 2007. Language indentification: How to distinguish similar languages? In *Information Technology Interfaces, 2007. ITI 2007. 29th International Conference on*, pages 541–546. IEEE.

Shervin Malmasi and Aoife Cahill. 2015. Measuring Feature Diversity in Native Language Identification. In *Proceedings of the Tenth Workshop on Innovative Use of NLP for Building Educational Applications*, Denver, Colorado, June. Association for Computational Linguistics.

Shervin Malmasi and Mark Dras. 2015a. Automatic Language Identification for Persian and Dari texts. In *Proceedings of the 14th Conference of the Pacific Association for Computational Linguistics (PACLING 2015)*, pages 59–64, Bali, Indonesia, May.

Shervin Malmasi and Mark Dras. 2015b. Large-scale Native Language Identification with Cross-Corpus Evaluation. In *Proceedings of NAACL-HLT 2015*, Denver, Colorado, June. Association for Computational Linguistics.

Shervin Malmasi, Sze-Meng Jojo Wong, and Mark Dras. 2013. NLI Shared Task 2013: MQ Submission. In *Proceedings of the Eighth Workshop on Innovative Use of NLP for Building Educational Applications*, pages 124–133, Atlanta, Georgia, June. Association for Computational Linguistics.

Shervin Malmasi, Eshrag Refaee, and Mark Dras. 2015a. Arabic Dialect Identification using a Parallel Multidialectal Corpus. In *Proceedings of the 14th Conference of the Pacific Association for Computational Linguistics (PACLING 2015)*, pages 209–217, Bali, Indonesia, May.

Shervin Malmasi, Joel Tetreault, and Mark Dras. 2015b. Oracle and Human Baselines for Native Language Identification. In *Proceedings of the Tenth Workshop on Innovative Use of NLP for Building Educational Applications*, Denver, Colorado, June. Association for Computational Linguistics.

Nikunj C Oza and Kagan Tumer. 2008. Classifier ensembles: Select real-world applications. *Information Fusion*, 9(1):4–20.

Robi Polikar. 2006. Ensemble based systems in decision making. *Circuits and Systems Magazine, IEEE*, 6(3):21–45.

Liling Tan, Marcos Zampieri, Nikola Ljubešic, and Jörg Tiedemann. 2014. Merging comparable data sources for the discrimination of similar languages: The dsl corpus collection. In *Proceedings of the 7th Workshop on Building and Using Comparable Corpora*, pages 11–15, Reykjavik, Iceland.

Jörg Tiedemann and Nikola Ljubešić. 2012. Efficient discrimination between closely related languages. In *Proceedings of COLING 2012*, pages 2619–2634.

Michał Woźniak, Manuel Graña, and Emilio Corchado. 2014. A survey of multiple classifier systems as hybrid systems. *Information Fusion*, 16:3–17.

George Udny Yule. 1912. On the methods of measuring association between two attributes. *Journal of the Royal Statistical Society*, pages 579–652.

Marcos Zampieri and Binyam Gebrekidan Gebre. 2012. Automatic identification of language varieties: The case of Portuguese. In *KONVENS2012-The 11th Conference on Natural Language Processing*, pages 233–237. Österreichischen Gesellschaft für Artificial Intelligende (ÖGAI).

Marcos Zampieri, Binyam Gebrekidan Gebre, and Sascha Diwersy. 2013. N-gram language models and POS distribution for the identification of Spanish varieties. In *Proceedings of TALN 2013*, pages 580–587.

Marcos Zampieri, Liling Tan, Nikola Ljubešic, and Jörg Tiedemann. 2014. A report on the DSL shared task 2014. *COLING 2014*, page 58.

Marcos Zampieri, Liling Tan, Nikola Ljubešić, Jörg Tiedemann, and Preslav Nakov. 2015. Overview of the dsl shared task 2015. In *Proceedings of the Joint Workshop on Language Technology for Closely Related Languages, Varieties and Dialects (LT4VarDial)*, Hissar, Bulgaria.

Discriminating similar languages with token-based backoff

Tommi Jauhiainen
University of Helsinki
@helsinki.fi

Heidi Jauhiainen
University of Helsinki
@helsinki.fi

Krister Lindén
University of Helsinki
@helsinki.fi

Abstract

In this paper we describe the language identification system built within the Finno-Ugric Languages and the Internet project for the Discriminating between Similar Languages (DSL) shared task in LT4VarDial workshop at RANLP-2015. The system reached fourth place in normal closed submissions (94.7% accuracy) and second place in closed submissions with the named entities blinded (93.0% accuracy).

1 Introduction

In the Finno-Ugric Languages and the Internet project[1], our aim is to harvest texts written in small Uralic languages from the internet. The project is funded by the Kone Foundation from its language program, which is especially targeted to support the research of Uralic languages (Kone Foundation, 2012). We are particularly interested in gathering material written in the smaller languages, instead of the three largest Uralic languages: Hungarian, Finnish and Estonian. As part of the project, we are developing methods for language identification which are needed to find the relevant texts among the billions of files we are downloading. At the moment, we have a list of 38 relevant languages based on the ISO 639-3 division of the Uralic languages (SIL, 2013). Some of the relevant languages, such as Livvi-Karelian and Ludic, two Finnic languages used in the north-western Russia, are very close to each other. However, the closeness between relevant languages is not as great a problem as the closeness between relevant and irrelevant languages. For example there are many dialectal variations of Finnish which are written differently from the standard Finnish and are actually closer in orthography to some of the very close languages, such as Tornedalen Finnish, than the standard written Finnish. This has led us to introduce separate language models for some of the Finnish dialects. An even greater problem for us is the large number of pages we have found which are written in a language not known to our language identifier (which at the moment has models for 395 languages and variants) or which consist mostly of lists of model abbreviations. Some of the character combinations used in the abbreviations tend to be quite common in some of the relevant languages and are therefore identified as such when the language identifier is forced to choose between languages it knows. Therefore, the opportunity given by the second version of the DSL shared task (Zampieri et al., 2015) to research unknown language detection has been very welcome.

[1] http://suki.ling.helsinki.fi

2 Language identification

The problem of discriminating similar languages given in the DSL shared task is an instance of monolingual language identification. The aim in monolingual language identification is to give one language label to a mystery text. This is different from multilingual language identification, where the mystery text can be labeled with several language labels. An extensive review of the work done in the area of discriminating between similar languages can be found in the report of the first edition of the DSL shared task (Zampieri et al., 2014).

The shared task also includes a group containing texts written in a set of unknown languages to which no training material is provided. Most existing language identifying methods can only categorize between languages they are trained for and do not have the ability to label the text as an unknown language. In order to detect the unknown language the methods usually need to have some

Proceedings of the Joint Workshop on Language Technology for Closely Related Languages, Varieties and Dialects, pages 44–51,
Hissar, Bulgaria, September 10, 2015. ©2015 Association for Computational Linguistics

notion of how well they are performing.

2.1 Token-based backoff

The basic language identifier used in this work was developed by Jauhiainen (2010) for his master's thesis. We call the method it uses the *token-based backoff*. In token-based backoff, the text is tokenized and the tokens t are numbered from 1 to the total number of tokens $|m^t|$ in the mystery text m, so that identical tokens can occur several times. The probability of each token $t_1 ... t_{|m^t|}$ for each language is calculated using the longest possible units and backing off to shorter units if needed. For example, if the token itself is not found in any of the language models it is divided into longest character n-grams used and the token gets the average of the scores of the n-grams in question. For each language l, each token t gets a score $S_{t,l}$ and the whole mystery text gets a score $S_{m,l}$ equal to the average of it's tokens as in (1).

$$S_{m,l} = \frac{S_{t_1,l} + S_{t_2,l} + ... + S_{t_{|m^t|},l}}{|m^t|} \quad (1)$$

In this way, each token in the mystery text is given an equal weight when deciding the language for the whole text. For example, the word "*the*" is given equal weight to the word "*village*". The token-based backoff was recently used successfully in determining the language set in multilingual documents by Jauhiainen et al. (2015).

2.2 Language models

The language models consist of units x and their scores $S_{x,l}$ for each language l. The scores S are negative logarithms of the relative frequencies of the units as in (2).

$$S_x = -\log_{10} (\text{relative frequency of } x) \quad (2)$$

The relative frequencies are calculated from the training data by dividing the number of units by the total number of units of the same type. If a unit is not found in the training data for some language a penalty value is used instead. The penalty value corresponds to giving every unseen unit a small relative frequency and thus it functions as a form of additive smoothing. The penalty values are optimized separately for each language using the development data. The optimization of the penalty values is done for one language after another and there is generally a more or less clear peak in the accuracy. In case several penalty values produce the highest accuracy, the smallest penalty value is chosen. In earlier experiments we have experimented with Lidstone smoothing, where the small relative frequency is also added to the relative frequencies of the seen units, but it proved out to produce slightly poorer results.

Character n-grams are formed from within the tokens so that the beginning and the end of the token are represented by a white-space. White space was omitted from the beginning of the first token where a special character marking the beginning of a text was used. The last token was treated similarly and the same special character was used to mark the end of the mystery text. The beginning and the end of the text were treated in similar way by Goutte et al. (2014).

No information spanning token boundaries were used this time. The types of units used in the system for the shared task in order of backing off are:

- Space-delimited tokens consisting of any characters (*A*)
- Tokens delimited by non-alphabetical characters with capital letters (*C*)
- Tokens delimited by non-alphabetical characters with the letters lowercased (*l*)
- Character n-grams of any character varying from the length of 8 to 1.

Examples of the token units can be seen in the Table 1 and character n-grams in the Table 2.

A	C	l
[_¡Que_]	[_Que_]	[_que_]
[_"La_]	[_La_]	[_la_]
[_Además,_]	[_Además_]	[_además_]
[_PP,_]	[_PP_]	[_pp_]

Table 1: Examples of token units from the Spanish language models. Underscore is used to represent a space character.

2.3 Unknown language detection

Unknown language detection is used by the system to decide whether the mystery text is written in one of the languages it knows or not. We are using the unknown language *xx* to denote any language not known by the language identifier. We

Length	*N*-grams from [_Además,_]
8	[_Además,], [Además,_]
7	[_Además], [Además,], [demás,_]
6	[_Ademá], [Además], [demás,] [emás,_]
5	[_Adem], [Ademá], [demás] [emás,], [más,_]
4	[_Ade], [Adem], [demá] [emás], [más,], [ás,_]
3	[_Ad], [Ade], [dem], [emá] [más], [ás,], [s,_]
2	[_A], [Ad], [de], [em] [má], [ás], [s,], [,_]
1	[_], [A], [d], [e], [m], [á], [s], [,], [_]

Table 2: Examples of character *n*-grams generated from the token [_Además,_]. Underscore is used to represent a space character.

used two methods to determine whether the language identified actually belonged to the unknown language *xx*. In both methods, the system first maps the mystery text into one of the languages it knows. After the first mapping the results are analyzed to detect the presence of an unknown language.

The first method is simply to look at the score given by the token-based backoff and reject identifications with too high scores. The unknown language *xx* is identified as the mystery language L_m, if the best score $S_{m,l}$ for the mystery text is higher than cut-off score C_l for the language l as in (3).

$$L_m = xx, \text{ if } S_{m,l} > C_l \tag{3}$$

The second one is to count how many of the lowercased words consisting of alphabetical characters in the mystery text are found in any of the language models of the language identifier. If the ratio of the words R_m is lower than the cut-off ratio R_l for the language with the best score $S_{m,l}$, the unknown language *xx* is chosen as in (4).

$$L_m = xx, \text{ if } R_m > R_l \tag{4}$$

The exact values for the cut-off ratios R_l and the cut-off scores C_l are determined individually for each language l. The development set is used to find out the values which produce the best combined recall for the language l and the unknown language *xx*.

3 Shared task

In the dataset of the shared task, there were 6 language groups with a total of 13 languages and the additional unknown language marked by *xx*. The unknown language *xx* is used to denote any language not belonging to the group of 13 languages. The goal was to build a system that could identify the language of the excerpts in the test set using only the information provided in the training and the development sets.

3.1 DSL corpus collection

The dataset for the shared task was the second version of the DSL corpus collection (DSLCC v. 2.0.). The training set consisted of 18000 labeled excerpts for each of the 13 languages. Each of the excerpts contained from 20 to 100 tokens and seemed to comprise mostly of a one complete sentence. Over 99% of the excerpts ended with a punctuation mark, a bracket or a quotation mark. The average number of tokens for each language can be seen in the Table 3. On the average the excerpts in Spanish had clearly more tokens than those of the other languages. The development set had 2000 labeled excerpts for each of the 13 languages as well as for the unknown language *xx*. The length of the excerpts in the development and training sets were comparable as can be seen in the Table 3. The average number of characters in the excerpts of the development set was 219. The number and the identity of the languages used in the excerpts of the unknown language *xx* were not known. Some of the excerpts in the unknown language *xx* were identified as Catalan and Slovenian by Google Translate[2], but also many other languages were present.

The test set A consisted of 14000 unlabeled excerpts from newspaper texts: 1000 excerpts for each of the 13 languages and 1000 excerpts for the unknown language. The test set B had the same number of unlabeled excerpts from newspaper texts, but all of the named entities had been substituted by place holders using a named entity recognizer. The following example excerpt is from the test set B:

- El #NE# #NE# #NE# #NE# asociación civil comprometida con el desarrollo económico y cultural de la ciudad, celebrará el 15° aniversario de su formación con una cena en el

[2]https://translate.google.com

Language l	Train.	Dev.
Croatian (hr)	29.6	29.7
Bosnian (bs)	30.7	30.9
Serbian (sr)	31.7	31.6
Malaysian (my)	30.3	30.2
Indonesian (id)	30.9	30.8
Czech (cz)	30.8	30.9
Slovakian (sk)	30.5	30.4
Portuguese (pt-PT)	33.0	33.3
Braz. Port. (pt-BR)	34.1	34.0
Spanish (es-ES)	55.7	56.4
Arg. Spa. (es-AR)	49.1	48.4
Bulgarian (bg)	29.6	29.7
Macedonian (mk)	30.2	30.0
Unknown (xx)	-	33.5

Table 3: The average number of tokens per excerpt in the training and the development sets for each language.

restaurant #NE# el jueves próximo desde las 20.30.

There was not a separate development set for the test set with the named entities blinded so the settings of our system were exactly the same on the test set A and B. Before running the language identifier on the test set B, we simply removed the place holders from the excerpts.

3.2 Language group identification

We followed the example given by the best performing system from the 2014 shared task (Goutte et al., 2014) and first used the system to discriminate between the six language groups. Development set was used to optimize the units used in the group identification phase and we ended up using character n-grams from 7 to 1 characters in length. The penalty value for unseen units was set at 6.7. With these settings, the system discriminated (at least on the third run, see below) between the groups perfectly on both the development and the test data, if we are not considering the unknown language. The average identification accuracy for individual languages with the development data was already 94.61% (*xx* not included). The Table 4 shows the accuracies with different unit combinations at this point. These combinations were more thoroughly run after the deadline for the shared task to show how much accuracy is gained by backing off to smaller units within the tokens. A small increase in overall accuracy was noticed when the penalty value was raised to 6.8 from 6.7. It would not have affected the end result of the system used in the shared task as the language identifier was only used to identify the language groups at this point and it did so perfectly already with the penalty value of 6.7.

Units	Pen.	Accuracy.
n-grams: 7 to 1	6.8	94.63%
n-grams: 7 to 1	6.7	94.61%
n-grams: 6 to 1	6.8	94.52%
n-grams: 8 to 1	6.7	94.50%
n-grams: 5 to 1	7.0	94.08%
$C + l + n$-grams: 8 to 1	6.4	94.31%
$l + n$-grams: 8 to 1	6.3	94.20%
$A + C + l + n$-grams: 8 to 1	6.4	94.15%
6-grams	6.8	93.98%
7-grams	6.6	93.80%
C	6.2	93.80%
5-grams	7.0	93.75%
l	6.2	93.70%
A	6.2	93.46%
n-grams: 4 to 1	7.2	92.97%
4-grams	7.2	92.88%
8-grams	6.2	92.81%
n-grams: 3 to 1	6.9	90.19%
3-grams	6.9	90.19%
n-grams: 2 to 1	7.6	83.22%
2-grams	7.6	83.22%
1-grams	6.5	73.63%

Table 4: The average accuracies for known languages using different unit combinations on the development set.

After the group of the mystery text was identified, the text was given to a group optimized version of the token-based language identifier. The units and the penalty value used within each group can be seen in the Table 5. In the token column A refers to tokens including all characters, C to tokens with only alphabetical characters and l to tokens with only lowercased alphabetical characters.

In the Table 5, we can see that the only time we use complete tokens for calculating the score is when we are discriminating between Malaysian and Indonesian. Ranaivo-Malançon (2006) used exclusive lists of words together with the formatting of numbers to decide whether the mystery text was written in Indonesian or Malaysian. The results of our experiments would also suggest that whole words are especially important when discriminating this pair of languages.

Group	Tokens	N-grams	Pen.
A-F	-	1-7	6.7
A (bs, hr, sr)	-	1-7	6.5
B (id, my)	A, C, l	1-8	7.0
C (cz, sk)	-	1-7	6.7
D (pt-PT, pt-BR)	-	1-7	6.7
E (es-ES, es-AR)	-	1-8	6.7
F (mk, bg)	-	1-7	6.7

Table 5: The language models used when discriminating within the language groups.

3.3 First run

The main difference between the first and the second runs is that in the first run, the language identifier was optimized so that it made as few positive errors with the unknown language xx as possible. Positive errors with the unknown language are errors where a language known to the language identifier is labeled as the unknown language xx. We wanted to continue developing unknown language detection methods (to be used one after another in a serialized manner) and once a positive error was made it was impossible to recover from it. We also wanted to see how high recall we would achieve with the known languages. When considering the overall accuracy, we did not believe that the results of the first run could compete with the results of the second run.

When we were optimizing the parameters, we took a look at the errors the language identifier made on the development set. After the optimization the unknown language xx was erroneously identified as one of the 13 languages known by the language identifier 324 times, while a known language was identified as unknown 4 times. With Malaysian we allowed the language identifier to make three 'errors' on the development set, as the sentences were actually in English:

- Daim not attending UMNO assembly, Tengku Adnan confirms © UTUSAN MELAYU (M) BHD, 46M Jalan Lima Off Jalan Chan Sow Lin, 55200 Kuala Lumpur.
- Complete signature forms should be mailed by August 23 to "Save Vui Kong" Campaign, Kuala Lumpur and Selangor Chinese Assembly Hall, 1, Jalan Maharajalela, 50150 Kuala Lumpur, Malaysia.
- Ishak said Jalan Perdana, Jalan Hishamuddin, Jalan Travers (opposite Keretapi Tanah Melayu Berhad), Jalan Mahameru and Jalan Istana Baru would be closed at 9.20 am for the cortege to be taken to Istana Negara.

Furthermore, we allowed it to make one error with Macedonian where the latter half of the sentence was actually written in Latin script instead of the Cyrillic normally used in Macedonian. This kind of errors in the dataset itself were not noticed in the test set.

The parameters used for the unknown language detection on the first run can be seen in the Table 6. R_l is the cut-off ratio and C_l is the cut-off score. The cut-off ratio for Slovak stayed as high as it did because the Slovak development set included some sentences where all the accents were omitted from the characters. We could have coped with this problem by creating separate language models for these languages with de-accented characters, but we did not have time to move further with this idea.

Language l	R_l	C_l
Croatian (hr)	32	5.4
Bosnian (bs)	35	5.0
Serbian (sr)	24	5.1
Malaysian (my)	20	5.3
Indonesian (id)	30	5.4
Czech (cz)	39	5.3
Slovakian (sk)	45	5.3
Portuguese (pt-PT)	25	4.9
Braz. Port. (pt-BR)	25	4.9
Spanish (es-ES)	12	6.5
Arg. Spa. (es-AR)	14	4.9
Bulgarian (bg)	30	5.3
Macedonian (mk)	35	5.1

Table 6: The cut-off ratios used with lowercased tokens and cut-off scores to judge the excerpt to be in the unknown language xx on the first run.

The first run achieved 93.87% accuracy on the development set and 93.73% accuracy on the test set.

3.4 Second run

The language models used for the second run were the same as for the first run and can be seen in the Table 5.

The unknown language detection parameters for the second run were optimized to reach the best overall identification accuracy. These ratios for unknown language detection differ considerably between languages as can be seen in the Table 7 which shows the ratios used for the second run.

Language l	R_l	C_l
Croatian (hr)	16	5.1
Bosnian (bs)	21	5.0
Serbian (sr)	23	5.1
Malaysian (my)	20	5.3
Indonesian (id)	30	5.4
Czech (cz)	39	5.3
Slovakian (sk)	45	5.2
Portuguese (pt-PT)	25	4.9
Braz. Port. (pt-BR)	25	4.9
Spanish (es-ES)	11	4.4
Arg. Spa. (es-AR)	14	4.9
Bulgarian (bg)	30	5.3
Macedonian (mk)	35	5.1

Table 7: The cut-off ratios used with lowercased tokens and cut-off scores to judge the excerpt to be in the unknown language xx for the second and the third runs.

In the development set, there was a clear tendency to identify Bosnian sentences as Croatian. We, therefore, experimented with giving a small bonus to Bosnian over Croatian. If the first identified language was Croatian but Bosnian came second within a score margin of 0.01, the text was identified as Bosnian. Twenty-three errors (out of 713 errors between Croatian, Bosnian and Serbian) were corrected by this very ad-hoc weight.

The unknown language was erroneously identified as one of the known languages 82 times. A known language was identified as the unknown language xx 58 times.

The second run achieved 94.61% accuracy on the development set and 94.36% accuracy on the test set.

3.5 Third run

The language models used for the third run were the same as for the first and second runs. The parameters for ratio and score cut-offs for determining the unknown language were the same for our third run as our second run and can be seen in the Table 7. The ad-hoc weight given to Bosnian in the second run was still used in the third run.

The third run included a special modifying addition αS_x to the scores S_x of individual character n-grams if they were not found in other languages within the group. The new score S'_x was calculated as in (5).

$$S'_x = S_x + \alpha S_x \qquad (5)$$

This was done for the groups A (bs, hr, sr) and E (es-ES, es-AR) only. We concentrated our efforts to finding ways to further the identification accuracy of the group A and did not have the time to find the optimal parameters for the other groups. We also did not expect to gain much in overall accuracy had we done so. The multipliers α used in the third run can be seen in the Table 8.

Found in	**Not found**	**Multiplier** α
hr	bs, sr	1.50
bs	sr, hr	2.00
sr	bs, hr	0.15
es-ES	es-AR	0.75
es-AR	es-ES	1.50

Table 8: The multipliers α for groups A and E.

The third run achieved 94.86% accuracy on the development set and 94.67% accuracy on the test set.

The confusion table for the third run on the test data with blinded named entities can be seen in the Table 9.

The within group accuracies for normal test set can be seen in the Table 10. It is clear that our system has a special problem with the group A, where our results are almost 6% lower than the best results of the 2014 shared task.

Group	**Accuracy.**
A-F	94.7%
A (bs, hr, sr)	87.7%
B (id, my)	99.7%
C (cz, sk)	99.8%
D (pt-PT, pt-BR)	92.4%
E (es-ES, es-AR)	90.4%
F (mk, bg)	99.8%
xx	98.2%

Table 10: The accuracies within the language groups for the third run on normal test set.

Comparison of the performance of our system to other systems which submitted results to the shared task can be found in the overview of the DSL Shared Task (Zampieri et al., 2015).

	bs	hr	sr	id	my	cz	sk	pt-PT	pt-BR	es-ES	es-AR	mk	bg	*xx*
bs	803	136	54	0	0	0	0	0	0	0	0	0	0	7
hr	76	905	7	0	0	0	0	0	0	0	0	0	0	12
sr	80	37	882	0	0	0	0	0	0	0	0	0	0	1
id	0	0	0	989	11	0	0	0	0	0	0	0	0	0
my	0	0	0	3	997	0	0	0	0	0	0	0	0	0
cz	0	0	0	0	0	1000	0	0	0	0	0	0	0	0
sk	0	0	0	0	0	0	997	0	0	0	0	0	0	3
pt-PT	0	0	0	0	0	0	0	869	131	0	0	0	0	0
pt-BR	0	0	0	0	0	0	0	103	897	0	0	0	0	0
es-ES	0	0	0	0	0	0	0	0	0	879	116	0	0	5
es-AR	0	0	0	0	0	0	0	0	0	158	842	0	0	0
mk	0	0	0	0	0	0	0	0	0	0	0	999	0	1
bg	0	0	0	0	0	0	0	0	0	0	0	0	999	1
xx	3	5	6	0	0	4	13	0	0	1	2	0	0	965

Table 9: The confusion table for the third run on the test set with the named entities blinded.

4 Discussion

The parameters for the language identifier and the language models used were exactly the same for the runs on development set and the corresponding test runs. We did not find the time to use the data in the development set as an additional training material for the actual test runs, even though we suspect it might have slightly improved the results on the test set.

The exact reason for the positive effect caused by the ad-hoc weight used with Bosnian and Croatian is not known. It is possible that the Bosnian training material is not as representative of the language as the Croatian. All data is biased to some extent and if the training data for a language identifier is biased differently from the data it is used on, situations such as this can arise.

The special character used to mark the beginning and the end of the text did not affect the results much. Using it gave a 0.03% increase in average individual language identification accuracy at the group identification phase.

After the shared task submissions, we optimized the multiplier α also for the other languages using the development set. Optimization resulted in a slight improvement with the Portuguese pair achieving 94.88% average accuracy on the development set. The optimized multipliers for the other languages were zero except for the Portuguese, as can be seen in the Table 11.

Acknowledgments

We thank the Kone Foundation for the funding that made possible the research presented in this paper. We also thank the anonymous reviewers for their extremely helpful suggestions.

Found in	Not found	Multiplier α
id	my	0.00
my	id	0.00
cz	sk	0.00
sk	cz	0.00
pt-PT	pt-BR	0.40
pt-BR	pt-PT	0.00
mk	bg	0.00
bg	mk	0.00

Table 11: The multipliers α for groups B, C, D and F.

References

Cyril Goutte, Serge Léger, and Marine Carpuat. 2014. The NRC System for Discriminating Similar Languages. In *Proceedings of the First Workshop on Applying NLP Tools to Similar Languages, Varieties and Dialects*, pages 139–145, Dublin, Ireland, August. Association for Computational Linguistics.

Tommi Jauhiainen, Krister Lindén, and Heidi Jauhiainen. 2015. Language Set Identification in Noisy Synthetic Multilingual Documents. In *Proceedings of the Computational Linguistics and Intelligent Text Processing 16th International Conference, CICLing 2015*, pages 633–643, Cairo.

Tommi Jauhiainen. 2010. Tekstin kielen automaattinen tunnistaminen. Master's thesis, University of Helsinki, Helsinki. http://urn.fi/URN:NBN:fi-fe201012223157.

Kone Foundation. 2012. The Language Programme 2012-2016. http://www.koneensaatio.fi/en.

Bali Ranaivo-Malançon. 2006. Automatic Identification of Close Languages–Case Study: Malay and Indonesian. *ECTI Transaction on Computer and Information Technology*, 2(2):126–133.

SIL. 2013. *ISO 639-3 Codes for the representation of names of languages*. SIL International. http://www.sil.org/iso639-3/.

Marcos Zampieri, Liling Tan, Nikola Ljubešić, and Jörg Tiedemann. 2014. A Report on the DSL Shared Task 2014. In *Proceedings of the First Workshop on Applying NLP Tools to Similar Languages, Varieties and Dialects*, pages 58–67, Dublin, Ireland, August. Association for Computational Linguistics.

Marcos Zampieri, Liling Tan, Nikola Ljubešić, Jörg Tiedemann, and Preslav Nakov. 2015. Overview of the DSL Shared Task 2015. In *Proceedings of the Joint Workshop on Language Technology for Closely Related Languages, Varieties and Dialects (LT4VarDial)*, Hissar, Bulgaria.

NLEL_UPV_Autoritas participation at Discrimination between Similar Languages (DSL) 2015 Shared Task

Raül Fabra-Boluda[1], **Francisco Rangel**[1,2], and **Paolo Rosso**[1]
[1] Natural Language Enginering Lab., Universitat Politècnica de València, Spain
[2] Autoritas Consulting, S.A., Spain
rfabra@dsic.upv.es, prosso@dsic.upv.es,
francisco.rangel@autoritas.es

Abstract

In this paper we describe the participation of the Natural Language Engineering Lab (NLEL) - Universitat Politècnica de València and Autoritas Consulting team in the Discrimination between Similar Languages (DSL) 2015 shared task. We have participated both in open and close submissions. Our system for the open submission performs in two steps. Firstly, we apply a language detector to identify the distinct groups corresponding to families of languages/dialects, and then we distinguish between varieties with a probabilistic method. For the close submission, we implemented our probabilistic method in a multi-class classifier for all the language varieties together. Although our results on the development set were quite promising (93.07% and 86.08% respectively), a software bug (that we have detected only after the submission) dropped considerably our results in the final testing.

1 Introduction

The automatic language identification task aims to determine the language of a given text. The performance on this task is pretty high with long texts (Shuyo, 2010), but it becomes harder when texts are shorter. This may occur in social media scenarios like Twitter (Carter et al., 2013). Furthermore, in social media we may want to go beyond the language scope to identify also dialects or varieties. The objective of the language variety identification is to determine the regional variety of a given language. For example, to know whether a Spanish text is Peninsular, Argentinian, Mexican, and so forth.

Language variety identification may be classified as an author profiling task. Author profiling aims at identifying the linguistic profile of an author on the basis of her writing style. The objective is to determine author's traits such as age, gender, native language, personality traits or language varieties, among others. It is noteworthy the interest in author profiling since 2013, as can be seen in the number of shared tasks: *i)* Age and gender identification at the Author Profiling task at PAN[1] at CLEF 2013 (Rangel et al., 2013) and 2014 (Rangel et al., 2014). In PAN 2015 (Rangel et al., 2015) personality recognition is also treated; *ii)* native language identification at BEA-8 workshop at NAACL-HLT 2013[2] (Tetreault et al., 2013); *iii)* personality recognition at ICWSM 2013[3]; *iv)* Workshop on Language Technology for Closely Related Languages and Language Variants at EMNLP2014[4]; *v)* VarDial Workshop at COLING 2014[5] - Applying NLP Tools to Similar Languages, Varieties and Dialects and *vi)* LT4VarDial - Joint Workshop on Language Technology for Closely Related Languages, Varieties and Dialect[6] (Zampieri et al., 2014).

DSL is a hot research topic. The authors in (Sadat et al., 2014) researched the identification of Arabic varieties in blogs and forums. They used character n-grams and Support Vector Machines, and reported accuracies between 70-80% in a 10-fold cross-validation evaluation. Similarly, in (Zampieri and Gebre, 2012) the authors collected 1.000 news articles in two Portuguese varieties: Portugal and Brazil. They used word n-grams and character n-grams and reported accuracies over 90% in a 50-50 split evaluation. They used language probability distributions with log-likelihood function for probability estimation.

[1] http://pan.webis.de
[2] https://sites.google.com/site/nlisharedtask2013/
[3] http://mypersonality.org/wiki/doku.php?id=wcpr13
[4] http://alt.qcri.org/LT4CloseLang/index.html
[5] http://corporavm.uni-koeln.de/vardial/sharedtask.html
[6] http://ttg.uni-saarland.de/lt4vardial2015/dsl.html

Proceedings of the Joint Workshop on Language Technology for Closely Related Languages, Varieties and Dialects, pages 52–58,
Hissar, Bulgaria, September 10, 2015.

In (Maier and Gómez-Rodrıguez, 2014), the authors collected tweets in four different Spanish varieties: Argentina, Colombia, Mexico and Spain. They used four types of features combined with a meta-classifier: character n-gram with frequency profiles, character n-gram language models, LZW compresssion and syllable-based language models. The reported accuracies were between 60-70% in a cross-validation evaluation.

It is also interesting to analyse the submitted systems to the LT4VarDial task. In the system presented in (Goutte et al., 2014) the authors approached the task in two steps. First, it predicted the language group with a 6-way probabilistic classifier. Then, the variety was predicted with a voting combination of discriminative classifiers. They used character and word n-grams and reported 95.71% of accuracy. The system presented in (Porta and Sancho, 2014) used a hierarchical classifier based on maximum-entropy classifiers. The first level predicted the language group and the second the language variety within the predicted group. They experimented with character and word n-grams, together with a list of words which exclusively belong to each language variety. The reported accuracy was 92.6%. The authors in (Purver, 2014) used linear Support Vector Machines with character and word n-grams. They analysed in depth how the cost parameter influenced the classification results, and reported an overall accuracy over 95% after fixing a bug. The system reported in (King et al., 2014) combined character and word n-grams with feature selection techniques such as Information Gain and Parallel Text Feature Extraction. The authors reported that Naive Bayes performed better than Support Vector Machines and Logistic Regression. In (Lui et al., 2014), the authors devoted their research to explore novel methods for DSL. They obtained their best result using their `langid.py` tool (Lui and Baldwin, 2012), with a 91.80% of accuracy.

Our interest in DSL goes beyond the use of features such as n-grams. Our objective is to better understand the linguistic differences between varieties as well as the relationship to other author profiling tasks. In (Franco-Salvador et al., 2015), we approached the DSL task with distributed representations. We also compared with Emograph (Rangel and Rosso, 2015a), a graph-based approach which obtained competitive accuracies with PAN datasets (Rangel and Rosso, 2015b) in the age and gender author profiling tasks. In this paper we describe our participation at the DSL 2015 shared task (Zampieri et al., 2015). We approached the task by proposing a probabilistic method which tries to capture lexical differences between varieties.

2 Identifying Language Varieties

We participated in both open and close tasks. Our objective was to compare the performance of our approach when dividing the identification in two steps against learning all varieties together.

For the open submission we have developed a two-step method. The first step consists in the identification of language groups by means of a language detector. We use the `ldig` language detector developed in (Shuyo, 2010). The author computed character n-grams from Wikipedia abstracts and used Naive Bayes as machine learning algorithm. The reported accuracies are about 99.1% for up to 53 languages.

In the second step, for each language group we obtain a series of probability measures for each term to belong to each variety in the group. Concretely, we calculate tf.idf weights for each term in the training set. With each weight, we calculate the probability as the relation between the sum of weights of the term belonging to the variety and the total sum of all its weights. In the end, we have the probability for each term to belong to each different variety of the language group. These probabilities were obtained from the training set. We must highlight that we learned a classifier for each language group, separately. Hence, the probabilities were computed locally for each group.

Once the language group of a new document is determined, to represent that document all its terms are computed with the previous probabilities for each language variety of such group. Then, we obtain six different measures from the computation of these probabilities: *1) Average*, computed as the sum of probabilities divided by the number of terms in the document; *2) Standard deviation*, computed as the root square of the sum of all probabilities minus the average; *3) Minimum probability*, the minimum of all probabilities computed for the document; *4) Maximum probability*, the maximum of all probabilities computed for the document; *5) Overall probability*, computed as the sum of all probabilities divided by the number of terms in the document and *6) Ratio*, computed as the number of terms appearing in the document divided by the number of terms in the vocabulary. We obtain these 6 measures for each variety. Hence, we represent each document with a total of 6 features (described above), multiplied by the number of languages/varieties of its detected group. For each group, we used a Bayesian Net classifier as machine learning method.

The whole process is as follows. To predict the language of a new text, first we detect its language with the `ldig` language detector. Once we know the language group, we calculate the six aforementioned measures for each variety in the group and predict the variety with a Bayesian Net classifier.

For the close submission we represented all varieties together. This implies to learn all the probabilities together and then to predict the right variety with a single multi-class classifier. In this case, we represent each document with a total of 84 features: the 6 features described above, multiplied by 14 languages/varieties of the task. As classification method, we used Naive Bayes due to performance issues in training phase.

3 Experimental Results

In this section we show the evaluation of the proposed methodology when participating in the DSL 2015 shared task. Firstly, the dataset and the evaluation methodology are described. Then, the official results are shown. We detected a bug that is also described in this section. Finally, we explain our participation in the open and close submissions respectively, and discuss a comparison between both submissions.

3.1 Dataset and Methodology

We used the DSLCC v.2.0 (Tan et al., 2014) dataset. The dataset contains sentences extracted from news in different languages and dialects. Table 1 summarises the different languages and varieties contained in the dataset. The group coded as *xx* is built with sentences of different languages.

The length of each sentence ranges from 20 to 100 tokens. For each language or dialect, this dataset contains 18.000 instances for training, 2.000 instances for development and 1.000 instances for each test set. A summary of the total number of instances is shown in Table 2. The dataset is composed of two test sets, A and B. They both contain the same instances, but the test B was processed with a Named Entity Recogniser (NER) to replace Named Entities (NE) by placeholders. This set is named NE blinded.

Group	Language	Code
South-Eastern Slavic	Bulgarian	bg
	Macedonian	mk
Spanish	Argentinian	es-AR
	Peninsular	es-ES
Portuguese	Brazilian	pt-BR
	European	pt-PT
South-Western Slavic	Bosnian	bs
	Croatian	hr
	Serbian	sr
Austranesian	Indonesian	id
	Malay	my
West Slavic	Czech	cz
	Slovak	sk
Other		xx

Table 1: Languages in the DSLCC v.2.0 dataset.

Training	Development	Test
252,000	28,000	14,000

Table 2: Number of instances per set.

We used the training set to learn probabilities and the corresponding machine learning models. We tested our methods with the development set using the Weka GUI[7] (Witten and Frank, 2005). We built a Java application to predict documents in the test set by using the models previously learned with Weka. In the following sections we explain the specific approach for both open and close submissions. We present comparative results among development, test A and test B. We also carried out a statistical significance test between results for both test sets. We used the following notation for confidence levels: * at 95% and ** at 99%

3.2 Task Results and Software Bug

Our results at the DSL task are shown in Table 3.

Open		Close	
Test A	Test B	Test A	Test B
91.84	89.56	64.04	62.78

Table 3: Identification accuracies for the open and close submission for tests A and B.

We detected a drop of accuracies between test and development. We reproduced the drop of accuracies by comparing results obtained with the

[7] http://www.cs.waikato.ac.nz/ml/weka/

Weka GUI and with our Java application in the development set. In Table 4 accuracies obtained by both methods are shown. The bug was present in our Java application. We did not compute properly the probabilities for the input set. Furthermore, some features were considered in wrong order.

Language	Weka GUI	Java App
es	87.75	86.60
pt	89.35	88.58
hr	83.63	79.96
id	99.43	99.42
all together	86.08	63.21

Table 4: Performance differences between Weka GUI and our Java application in the development set.

We could not fix the bug before submission time, and therefore our final results were much lower than we have expected. This is especially important in the close submission where the accuracy dropped more than 20%. In the following sections we analyse results with the error fixed.

3.3 Open Submission

We approached the open submission as a two-step process. Firstly, we used the `ldig` language detector to obtain the language group. The `ldig` detector was trained from the xml Wikipedia abstracts. We do not explicitly set any language group. Instead, the `ldig` language detector detects similar languages/dialects as a single language. We profit this fact to establish the language groups. The accuracy of this step for the development set is shown in Table 5.

Languages/Varieties	Language Group	Accuracy
bg	bg	99.80
mk	mk	100.00
es-AR, es-ES	es	99.96
pt-BR, pt-PT	pt	99.72
hr, bs, sr	hr	99.73
id, my	id	99.92
cz	cz	99.63
sk	sk	99.65
other languages	xx	99.90
	overall	99.81

Table 5: Identification accuracies of the `ldig` language detector in the development set.

In this step, we could detect Bulgarian (*bg*), Czech (*cz*), Macedonian (*mk*) and Slovak (*sk*). With respect to the other varieties, they were detected as follows: South-Western Slavic languages (Croatian, Bosnian and Serbian) were detected as Croatian (*hr*); Austranesian languages (Indonesian and Malay) were detected as Indonesian (*id*); and Spanish languages (Peninsular and Argentinian) and Portuguese languages (European and Brazilian) as their respective groups (*es* and *pt*). We classified as *xx* all the rest. Once the language group was identified, we applied our probabilistic method to detect the corresponding variety. Results for the development, test and NE blinded test sets are shown in Table 6.

Language	Accuracy		
	Devel.	Test A	Test B
bg*	99.80	99.90	99.80
mk*	100.00	99.90	100.00
es-ES	88.00	84.70	79.50
es-AR*	87.50	88.00	87.70
pt-PT	88.60	87.40	94.00
pt-BR	90.10	90.03	68.50
bs*	78.35	78.00	74.40
hr*	86.15	85.80	85.40
sr**	86.40	86.40	82.70
id	99.40	99.40	92.90
my*	99.45	99.20	99.50
cz*	99.70	99.80	99.40
sk*	99.60	99.30	99.60
xx*	99.90	99.90	99.70
overall	93.07	92.71	90.22

Table 6: Identification accuracies for the open submission for development, test, and NE blinded test.

Results for groups with only one language (*bg*, *mk*, *cz*, *sk*) show accuracies over 99% for both development and test sets. Accuracies for groups with more than one variety are quite lower. But this is not the case of Austronesian (*id*) where the achieved results are greater than 99% except for the *id* variety in the NE blinded test. The worst results were obtained for South-Western Slavic (*hr*) where the classifier should discriminate among three classes. The significance test shows us that our method is quite robust against blinded Named Entities in case of South-Western Slavic varieties (*bs*, *hr* and *sr*), Malay (*my*) and Argentinian Spanish (*es-AR*).

3.4 Close Submission

In the close submission we trained from the whole training set a multi-class classifier for the set of 14 different languages. The results are summarised in Table 7.

We can see that overall results for test B (72.11%) are much lower than for test A (85.57%) and development (86.08%). In this line, results for most languages are significantly different, except

Language	Accuracy		
	Devel.	Test A	Test B
bg	98.15	97.50	95.10
mk*	98.95	98.20	98.20
es-ES	87.55	84.80	48.70
es-AR**	67.05	70.00	74.10
pt-PT	82.15	81.20	58.30
pt-BR	72.45	72.50	65.90
bs	55.70	54.30	86.20
hr	80.85	78.88	13.10
sr	74.40	74.70	7.80
id	97.75	97.60	92.00
my	94.25	93.60	97.60
cz	98.45	98.40	94.40
sk	98.80	97.60	79.30
xx*	98.55	98.50	98.80
overall	86.08	85.57	72.11

Table 7: Identification accuracies for the close submission for development, test, and NE blinded test.

for the Argentinian Spanish (*es-AR*), Macedonian (*mk*) and Other (*xx*) groups. This may be due to the probabilities of terms corresponding to NE, which may cause confusion between some varieties.

3.5 Comparison between Methods

In Table 8, the comparative results between open and close approaches in the development set are shown. It is noteworthy that both approaches obtained lower results with the same groups (*es*, *pt* and *hr*). Regarding groups with only one language (*bg*, *mk*, *cz* and *sk*), both approaches obtained accuracies over 95%. We carried out the significance test but we cannot assert that any system performs equal for both open and close submissions. Therefore, we can conclude that the two-step method for the open submission was more accurate than dealing with all the varieties together.

Group	Accuracy	
	Open	Close
bg	99.80	98.15
mk	100.0	98.95
es	87.75	77.30
pt	89.35	77.30
hr	83.63	70.32
id	99.43	96.0
cz	99.70	98.45
sk	99.60	98.80
xx	99.90	98.55
overall	93.07	86.08

Table 8: Identification accuracies for the open and close submissions in development set.

4 Conclusions

In this work we presented the NLEL_UPV_Autoritas team participation at the DSL shared task. We submitted runs for both open and close tasks, for both normal and NE blinded tests. For the open submission, we developed a two-step system: in the first step we detected the language group and then the specific variety. For the close submission, we approached the task as a multi-class classification problem with all the varieties together.

We detected a software bug that dropped our results significantly in the testing phase. We fixed the bug and presented comparative results among development, test A and test B. We can conclude that approaching the task in two steps allows for obtaining better results than identifying all varieties together. Other teams approached the DSL 2014 shared task with two-step classification systems, obtaining good results. In this vein, Goutte et al. (2014) obtained the highest overall accuracy (95.71%) by predicting first the language group with a probabilistic generative classifier, and then predicting the variety within that group with a voting combination of classifiers. Porta and Sancho (2014) also predicted first the group and then the variety, with a hierarchical classifier based on maximum-entropy classifiers. They obtained an overall accuracy of 92.6%. Regarding varieties, the hardest prediction came with South-Western Slavic language, followed by Spanish and Portuguese. The Austranesian group was properly identified with both approaches. Groups composed by only one language obtained higher accuracies both in open and close approaches.

As future work we plan to approach the task implementing our own language detector. Moreover, we would like to investigate how to improve the accuracy in more similar languages than South-Western Slavic, Spanish or Portuguese, and to better deal with Named Entities.

Acknowledgement

The work of the second author was partially funded by Autoritas Consulting SA and by Spanish Ministry of Economics under grant ECOPORTUNITY IPT-2012-1220-430000. The work of the third author has been carried out within the framework of the European Commission WIQEI IRSES (no. 269180) and DIANA - Finding Hidden Knowledge in Texts (TIN2012-38603-C02) projects, and the VLC/CAMPUS Microcluster on Multimodal Interaction in Intelligent Systems.

References

Simon Carter, Wouter Weerkamp, and Manos Tsagkias. 2013. Microblog language identification: Overcoming the limitations of short, unedited and idiomatic text. *Language Resources and Evaluation*, 47(1):195–215.

Marc Franco-Salvador, Francisco Rangel, Paolo Rosso, Mariona Taulé, and M. Antònia Martí. 2015. Language variety identification using distributed representations of words and documents. In *Proceeding of the 6th International Conference of CLEF on Experimental IR meets Multilinguality, Multimodality, and Interaction (CLEF 2015)*, volume LNCS(9283). Springer-Verlag.

Cyril Goutte, Serge Léger, and Marine Carpuat. 2014. The nrc system for discriminating similar languages. In *Proceedings of the First Workshop on Applying NLP Tools to Similar Languages, Varieties and Dialects*, pages 139–145, Dublin, Ireland, August. Association for Computational Linguistics.

Ben King, Dragomir Radev, and Steven Abney. 2014. Experiments in sentence language identification with groups of similar languages. In *Proceedings of the First Workshop on Applying NLP Tools to Similar Languages, Varieties and Dialects*, pages 146–154, Dublin, Ireland, August. Association for Computational Linguistics.

Marco Lui and Timothy Baldwin. 2012. langid. py: An off-the-shelf language identification tool. In *Proceedings of the ACL 2012 system demonstrations*, pages 25–30. Association for Computational Linguistics.

Marco Lui, Ned Letcher, Oliver Adams, Long Duong, Paul Cook, and Timothy Baldwin. 2014. Exploring methods and resources for discriminating similar languages. In *Proceedings of the First Workshop on Applying NLP Tools to Similar Languages, Varieties and Dialects*, pages 129–138, Dublin, Ireland, August. Association for Computational Linguistics.

Wolfgang Maier and Carlos Gómez-Rodrıguez. 2014. Language variety identification in spanish tweets. *LT4CloseLang 2014*, page 25.

Jordi Porta and José-Luis Sancho. 2014. Using maximum entropy models to discriminate between similar languages and varieties. In *Proceedings of the First Workshop on Applying NLP Tools to Similar Languages, Varieties and Dialects*, pages 120–128, Dublin, Ireland, August. Association for Computational Linguistics.

Matthew Purver. 2014. A simple baseline for discriminating similar languages. In *Proceedings of the First Workshop on Applying NLP Tools to Similar Languages, Varieties and Dialects*, pages 155–160, Dublin, Ireland, August. Association for Computational Linguistics.

Francisco Rangel and Paolo Rosso. 2015a. On the impact of emotions on author profiling. *Information Processing & Management*, (In press) doi: 10.1016/j.ipm.2015.06.003.

Francisco Rangel and Paolo Rosso. 2015b. On the multilingual and genre robustness of emographs for author profiling in social media. In *Proceeding of the 6th International Conference of CLEF on Experimental IR meets Multilinguality, Multimodality, and Interaction (CLEF 2015)*, volume LNCS(9283). Springer-Verlag.

Francisco Rangel, Paolo Rosso, Moshe Moshe Koppel, Efstathios Stamatatos, and Giacomo Inches. 2013. Overview of the author profiling task at pan 2013. In *Forner P., Navigli R., Tufis D.(Eds.), Notebook Papers of CLEF 2013 LABs and Workshops. CEUR-WS.org, vol. 1179.*

Francisco Rangel, Paolo Rosso, Irina Chugur, Martin Potthast, Martin Trenkmann, Benno Stein, Ben Verhoeven, and Walter Daelemans. 2014. Overview of the 2nd author profiling task at pan 2014. In *Cappellato L., Ferro N., Halvey M., Kraaij W. (Eds.) CLEF 2014 Labs and Workshops, Notebook Papers. CEUR-WS.org, vol. 1180.*

Francisco Rangel, Fabio Celli, Paolo Rosso, Martin Potthast, Benno Stein, and Walter Daelemans. 2015. Overview of the 3rd author profiling task at pan 2015. In *Cappellato L., Ferro N., Gareth J. and San Juan E. (Eds). CLEF 2015 Labs and Workshops, Notebook Papers. CEUR-WS.org.*

Fatiha Sadat, Farnazeh Kazemi, and Atefeh Farzindar. 2014. Automatic identification of arabic language varieties and dialects in social media. *SocialNLP 2014*, page 22.

Nakatani Shuyo. 2010. Language detection library for java. http://code.google.com/p/language-detection/.

Liling Tan, Marcos Zampieri, Nikola Ljubešic, and Jörg Tiedemann. 2014. Merging comparable data sources for the discrimination of similar languages: The dsl corpus collection. In *Proceedings of the 7th Workshop on Building and Using Comparable Corpora*, pages 11–15, Reykjavik, Iceland.

Joel Tetreault, Daniel Blanchard, and Aoife Cahill. 2013. A report on the first native language identification shared task. In *Proceedings of the Eighth Workshop on Innovative Use of NLP for Building Educational Applications*, pages 48–57.

Ian H Witten and Eibe Frank. 2005. *Data Mining: Practical machine learning tools and techniques.* Morgan Kaufmann.

Marcos Zampieri and Binyam Gebrekidan Gebre. 2012. Automatic identification of language varieties: The case of portuguese. In *KONVENS2012-The 11th Conference on Natural Language Processing*, pages 233–237. Österreichischen Gesellschaft für Artificial Intelligende (ÖGAI).

Marcos Zampieri, Liling Tan, Nikola Ljubešić, and Jörg Tiedemann. 2014. A report on the dsl shared task 2014. In *Proceedings of the First Workshop on Applying NLP Tools to Similar Languages, Varieties and Dialects*, pages 58–67, Dublin, Ireland, August. Association for Computational Linguistics.

Marcos Zampieri, Liling Tan, Nikola Ljubešić, Jörg Tiedemann, and Preslav Nakov. 2015. Overview of the dsl shared task 2015. In *Proceedings of the Joint Workshop on Language Technology for Closely Related Languages, Varieties and Dialects (LT4VarDial)*, Hissar, Bulgaria.

Discriminating between Similar Languages Using PPM

Victoria Bobicev
Technical University of Moldova
victoria_bobicev@rol.md

Abstract

The paper presents the results of participation of Bobicev team in DSL (Discriminating Similar Languages) shared task 2015. It describes the use of PPM (Prediction by Partial Matching) for language discrimination. The accuracy of the presented system was equal to 94.14% for the first set and 92.22% for the second set. The results were scored as the 4th for the first task and 5th for the second task, the best results being 95.54% and 94.01% respectively.

1 Introduction

The task of language identification is the problem of detection what language a document is written in. The task seems to be relatively easy and many statistical methods achieve relatively high accuracy (more than 95%) for language detection. However, the good results obtained in the laboratory simplified conditions become worse in the real word circumstances. Very short documents (such as tweets), fragments of various languages in one text, documents written in similar languages – here are just some difficulties encountered by the language detection systems. The present paper describes use of PPM (prediction by Partial Matching) statistical method for language discrimination task.

The accuracy of the presented system for the DSL 2015[1] (Discriminating Similar Languages) shared task (Zampieri et al., 2015) was equal to 94.14% for the first set; 92.22% for the second set respectively. The results were scored as the 4th for the first task and 5th for the second task, the best results being 95.54% and 94.01% respectively.

The advantage of the proposed method is its relative simplicity. The method operates with sequences of characters or even bytes, thus it does not need to tokenize or preprocess the analyzed text in any way. This also makes it relatively fast in training and text processing.

The paper is organized as follows: the next part gives a short overview of the related work; section 3 contains the system description and explanations how it was used for the task at hand; section 4 includes task (4.2) and data presentation (4.1), experiments and the obtained results (4.3, 4.4). Finally, a discussion concludes the paper.

2 Related work

The first DSL (Discriminating Similar Languages) shared task has been organized in 2014 and the task participants presented their systems at the VarDial workshop at COLING 2014. The DSL corpus collection was created for the evaluation by merging three comparable corpora of similar languages and language varieties. Tan et al. (2014) described the process of the corpus creation and reported the performance of up to 87.4% accuracy for the baseline discrimination experiments. In the overall report for this task (Zampieri, 2014) the organizers presented the results of 8 final submissions. All participants that described their systems used statistical methods such as Naïve Bayes, SVM, Max. Ent. and other. All of them used words and character n-grams as features.

The shared task organizers mentioned that the problem of similar languages discrimination was similar to the problem proposed in the Native Language Identification (NLI) shared task (Tetreault et al., 2013) where participants were provided English essays written by foreign students of 11 different mother tongues and had to identify the native language of the writer of each text. The differences between very similar languages can be as subtle as in case of the same language used by different people.

Ljubešić & Kranjčić (2014) presented the work on discrimination between tweets written in very similar languages, namely Bosnian, Croatian,

[1] http://ttg.uni-saarland.de/lt4vardial2015/dsl.html

Proceedings of the Joint Workshop on Language Technology for Closely Related Languages, Varieties and Dialects, pages 59–65,
Hissar, Bulgaria, September 10, 2015. ©2015 Association for Computational Linguistics

Montenegrin and Serbian and testing a number of statistical methods and various features such as tokens, character 3-grams and 6-grams obtained the best accuracy of ~97%. The authors mentioned that in some cases the text can be written in a mixture of languages either similar ones or with fragments of English or other widely used languages.
Baldwin & Lui (2010) analyzed the influence of number of discriminated languages, the amount of training data and the length of documents on the accuracy of document language detection. They experimented with three relatively difficult corpora: (1) EUROGOV containing relatively longer documents, all in a single encoding, spread evenly across a relatively small number (10) of Western European languages; (2) TCL (Thai Computational Linguistics Laboratory) with a larger number of languages (60) across a wider range of language families, with shorter documents and a range of character encodings; (3) WIKIPEDIA: a slightly larger number of languages (67), a single encoding, and shorter documents. Testing a number of statistical methods and using bytes, codepoints (pairs of bytes), uni-, bi-, and trigrams as features they obtained the best accuracy 0.987 for EuroGOV; 0.977 for TCL and 0.671 for Wikipedia. Experimenting with the n-grams of various length they managed to rise the accuracy to 0.729 for Wikipedia. The authors found that longer documents were easier for detection however they often contained fragments in other languages different than the main language of the document.

Malmasi (2015) presented the work on discriminating two similar languages: Persian and Dari achieving the 96% accuracy using character and word n-grams on the collected corpus of 28k sentences (14k per-language). Out-of-domain cross-corpus evaluation, however, achieved 87% accuracy in classifying 79k sentences from the Uppsala Persian Corpus.

3 System description

We explored the PPM (Prediction by Partial Matching) model for automatic text language detection. Prediction by partial matching (PPM) is an adaptive finite-context method for text compression that is a back-off smoothing technique for finite-order Markov models (Bratko et al., 2006). It obtains all information from the original data, without feature engineering, it is easy to implement and relatively fast. PPM produces a language model and can be used in a probabilistic text classifier. Treating a text as a string of characters, the character-based PPM avoids defining word boundaries; it deals with different types of documents in a uniform way. It can work with texts in any language and be applied to diverse types of classification.

PPM is based on conditional probabilities of the upcoming symbol given several previous symbols. A blending strategy for combining context predictions is to assign a weight to each context model, and then calculate the weighted sum of the probabilities:

$$P(x) = \sum_{i=1}^{m} \lambda_i p_i(x), \qquad (1)$$

where λ_i and p_i are weights and probabilities assigned to each order *i* $(i=1...m)$.

For example, the probability of character '***m***' in context of the word '***algorithm***' is calculated as a sum of conditional probabilities dependent on different context lengths up to the limited maximal length:

$$P_{PPM}('m') = \lambda_5 \cdot P('m' \mid 'orith') + \lambda_4 \cdot P('m' \mid 'rith') + \\ + \lambda_3 \cdot P('m' \mid 'ith') + \lambda_2 \cdot P('m' \mid 'th') + \\ + \lambda_1 \cdot P('m' \mid 'h') + + \lambda_0 \cdot P('m') + \lambda_{-1} \cdot P('esc'),$$

where

λ_i $(i = 1...5)$ is the normalization weight;

5 is the maximal length of the context;

P('esc') is so called 'escape' probability, the probability of an unknown character.

PPM is a special case of the general blending strategy. The PPM models use an escape mechanism to combine the predictions of all contexts of all lengths starting with the maximal length m and ending with the context -1.

The PPM escape mechanism is more practical to implement than weighted blending. In the general weighted blending the weighted coefficients have to be estimated and this requires additional calculations. In PPM the escape mechanism replaces the coefficients. The estimation of a character probability starts with the context of the maximal length m. If the given character probability can be estimated with this context, this probability is used for the character. If this context has not appeared and the character probability cannot be estimated with the longest context m, the method moves to the shorter context m-1 using the escape mechanism. If the shorter context also cannot be used, the method moves to the shorter context. Context -1 ensure that this happens even in the case when the character itself is unknown in the model.

There are several versions of the PPM algorithm depending on the way the escape probability for each context is estimated. In our implementation, we used the escape method C, named PPMC; more details can be found in (Bobicev, 2007). The maximal length of a context equal to 5 in PPM model was proven to be optimal for text compression (Teahan, 1998). In all our experiments with character-based PPM model we used maximal length of a context equal to 5; thus our method is PPMC5.

As a compression algorithm PPM is based on the notion of *entropy* introduced as a measure of a message uncertainty (Shannon, 1948):

$$H_d = -\sum_{i=1}^{n} p(x_i)\log p(x_i) \quad (2)$$

where

H_d – entropy of text d;

$p(x_i)$ - probability of character x_i $(i = 1...n)$ for all characters in the text d.

Cross-entropy is the entropy calculated for a text if the probabilities of its characters have been estimated on another text (Teahan, 1998):

$$H_d^m = -\sum_{i=1}^{n} p^m(x_i)\log p^m(x_i) \quad (3)$$

where

n is the number of symbols in a text d,

$H_d{}^m$ is the entropy of the text d obtained by model m,

$p^m(x_i)$ is a probability of a symbol x_i in the text d obtained by model m.

The cross-entropy between two texts is greater than the entropy of a text itself, because probabilities of characters in diverse texts are different:

$$H_d^m \geq H_d \quad (4)$$

The cross-entropy can be used as a measure for document similarity; the lower cross-entropy for two texts is, the more similar they are. Hence, if several statistical models had been created using documents that belong to different classes and cross-entropies are calculated for an unknown text on the basis of each model, the lowest value of cross-entropy indicates the class of the unknown text. In this way cross-entropy is used for text classification.

In practical tasks the per-character entropy is used in order to avoid the influence of document length in the process of entropy comparison:

$$H_L = \frac{1}{n}\left(-\sum_{i=1}^{n} p(x_i)\log p(x_i)\right)$$

Our utility function for text classification was per-character cross-entropy of the test document while the probabilities were estimated on the base of the known classes of documents.

On the training step, we created PPMC5 models for each class of documents; on the testing step, we evaluated cross-entropy of previously unseen texts using models for each class. Thus, cross-entropy was used as similarity metrics; the lowest value of cross-entropy indicated the class of the unknown text.

There are several variations of PPM method. One possible is to use not all characters from the text but only some of them, for example, only alphanumeric characters or only letters. In our case when we have to discriminate the languages not all characters in text seem important. We probably do not need any figures or special characters but the punctuation may be the specific for the language.

Another variation is the word-based PPM (Bobicev, 2006). For some tasks words can be more indicative text features than character sequences. That's why we decided to try both character-based and word-based models for language identification. In the case of word-based PPM, the context is only one word and an example for the formula (1) looks like the following:

$P_{PPM}(\text{'}word_i\text{'}) = \lambda_1 \cdot P(\text{'}word_i\text{'} \mid \text{'}word_{i-1}\text{'}) +$
$+ \lambda_0 \cdot P(\text{'}word_i\text{'}) + \lambda_{-1} \cdot P(\text{'esc'})$,

where

$word_i$ is the current word;

$word_{i-1}$ is the previous word.

This model is coded as PPMC1 because of the same C escape method and one length context used for probability estimation.

4 Experiments description

The experiments were carried out during the DSL 2015 shared task event. The first set of the experiments was performed on the base of training data released by the organisers in May 2015. The second set consisted of evaluation runs on test data released in June and the results for these experiments were provided by the organizers.

4.1 The Data Description

For the DSL shared task 2015 edition, the organizers released two new versions of the DSL corpus collection[2] (DSLCC), the version 2.0 and 2.1[3]. The version 2.0 is the standard shared task training material whereas the version 2.1 can be

[2] https://bitbucket.org/alvations/dslsharedtask2014
[3] http://ttg.uni-saarland.de/lt4vardial2015/dsl.html

used for the unshared task track or as additional training material. The collection is described in (Tan et al., 2014).

In 2015, apart from the similar languages and varieties the training and test sets were also including texts from other languages to emulate a real-world language identification scenario. Finally, the two released versions were the following:

1) DSLCC version 2.0. contained Bulgarian, Macedonian, Serbian, Croatian, Bosnian, Czech, Slovak, Argentinian Spanish, Peninsular Spanish, Brazilian Portuguese, European Portuguese, Malay, Indonesian and a group containing texts written in a set of other languages.

2) DSLCC version 2.1. contained all the DSLCC version 2.0. plus Mexican Spanish and Macanese Portuguese.

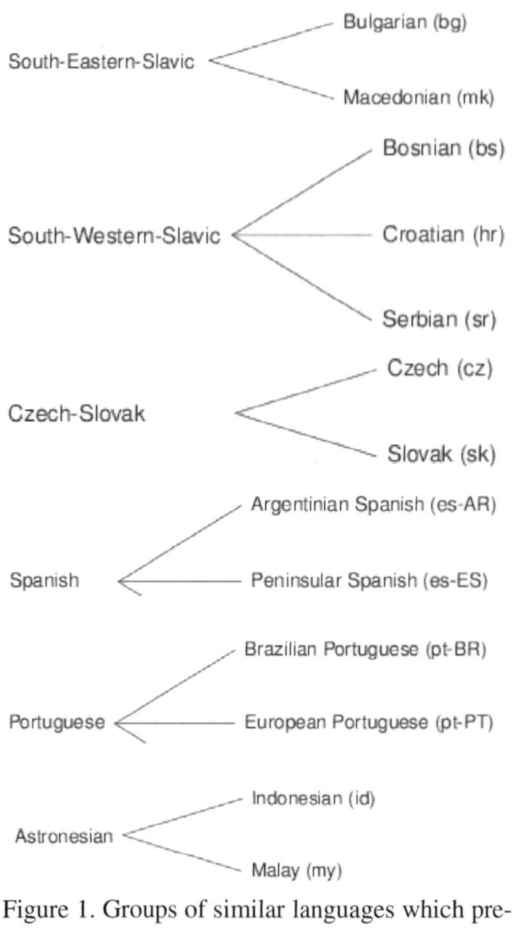

Figure 1. Groups of similar languages which presented difficulties in the process of language identification.

The corpus contained 20,000 instances per language (18,000 training + 2,000 development). Each instance was an excerpt extracted from journalistic texts containing 20 to 100 tokens and tagged with the country of origin of the text. The groups of similar languages are presented in figure 1.

4.2 The task description

For the testing phase two test sets (A and B) have been released. Each of them contained 1,000 unidentified instances of each language to be classified according to the country of origin. These instances contained also instances of texts from the other languages than those presented in the figure similarly to the training set DSLCC version 2.0.

Test set A contained original unmodified newspaper texts. Test set B contained modified newspapers texts processed with NER taggers to substitute named entities for place holders.

Participants had to return their results in up to 2 days after the release of the test sets. Scores were calculated according to the systems' accuracy in identifying the country of origin of the text. Two kinds of submissions were allowed:

1) Closed submission: Using only the training corpus provided by the DSL shared task (DSLCC v.2.0).

2) Open submission: Using any corpus for training including or not the DSLCC v.2.0.

We participated only in closed submission using just the corpus DSLCC v.2.0.

4.3 The first set of the experiments

In order to evaluate the PPM method for the task we used 10-fold cross-validation on the all provided training data. Initially, we excluded the instances marked as xx with the unknown languages to see how the method performed on the known sets. Thus, for each step we used 1800 instances of each language for training and 200 instances of each language for test.

We used character-based PPM5 in the first set of the experiments. The first experiment was performed using only letters for training, all other characters were ignored.

metrics	experiment	
	1st	2nd
microaverage F-score	0.928	0.933
macroaverage Precision	0.929	0.934
macroaverage Recall	0.928	0.933
macroaverage F-score	0.928	0.933

Table 1: The results for the first and the second experiments using letter and character based PPM5

In the second experiment we used all characters from the texts; all letters were converted in lower case. The results for the first and the second experiments are presented in table 1.

Thus, we obtained slightly better results in case when all characters from the texts were used.

The next experiment was performed using word-based PPM1 described in the previous section. Its results were worse than for character based PPM5.

Next, we experimented with the unknown languages marked as xx. There were several languages and thus, they did not present one uniform class of texts. While the entropy for the texts written in the same language was in average 2 ± 0.5 bit/symbol, for the different languages the average entropy varied from 4 to even 12 bit/symbol.

We considered two options of the unknown languages classification:

- A threshold for these languages was used. If the smallest entropy of a test text on the base of all models is bigger than a threshold we considered that text as not written in any of 13 known languages and hence, as unknown one and marked as xx. In this case we created models only on 13 known classes of languages.
- All text marked with xx were treated as one more class. In this case, 14 models were created, including a model for xx class and the standard procedure was applied. Each test document was attributed to the class for which it has the lowest entropy.

metrics	experiment	
	1st	2nd
microaverage F-score	0.922	0.938
macroaverage Precision	0.926	0.939
macroaverage Recall	0.922	0.938
macroaverage F-score	0.924	0.939

Table 2: The results for the first and the second experiments with the unknown texts marked as xx

The obtained results are presented in table 2. Thus, the second option when all the documents written in the unknown languages were treated as the one class was better. More than that, this result was even better than the pure classification of 13 known languages. This indicates that xx class was distinguished fairly well.

4.4 The second set of the experiments

The second set of the experiments was performed on the base of the test data released by the organizers of DSL shared task in June 2015.

These DSL Test Sets are part of the DSLCC v2.0, they comprise news data from various corpora to emulate the diverse news content across different languages and varieties.

Two types of test data were released:

•The first test set that contained 14,000 unchanged sentences for 13 anguages/varieties and others (bg, bs, cz, es-AR, es-ES, hr, id, mk, my, pt-BR, pt-PT, sk, sr, xx).

•The second test that contained 14,000 sentences with that had blinded Named Entities. In these texts, the Named Entities (NEs) have been replaced by placeholders; a #NE# instead of a named entity.

An example of such sentence is:

The initial sentence: La cinta, que hoy se estrena en nuestro país, competirá contra Hors la Loi, de Argelia, Dogtooth, de Grecia, Incendies, de Canadá, Life above all , de Sudáfrica, y con la ganadora del Globo de Oro, In A Better World, de Dinamarca.

The sentence with blinded NE: La cinta, que hoy se estrena en nuestro país, competirá contra #NE# la #NE# , de #NE# , #NE# , de #NE# , #NE# , de #NE# á, #NE# above all , de #NE# , y con la ganadora del #NE# de #NE# , #NE# A #NE# #NE# , de #NE# .

The participants were allowed to submit only 3 runs for closed and/or 3 runs for open task for both test sets.

We submitted only one run for each test set using PPM5 character based method using all characters from the text as this option demonstrated the best results in the first set of experiments. While experimenting with the second test set with blinded NE we simply removed #NE# fragments and worked with the rest of the text. Thus, the example of the sentence presented above would look as follows: La cinta, que hoy se estrena en nuestro país, competirá contra la , de , , de , , de á, above all , de , y con la ganadora del de , A , de .

The overall accuracies in these experiments were calculated by the organizers as such:

overall accuracy = sum(TP) / #sents

where:

TP = True Positive for all languages/varieties;

#sents = total number of documents in evaluation dataset.

The accuracy for the first task was equal to 94.14; for the second set it was 92.22. The results were scored as the 4th for the first task and 5th for the second task, the best results being 95.54 and 94.01 respectively.

5 Discussion

The challenges are an excellent way to examine the problem at hand from the various points of view. The challenge organizer's work is very important in this context. The saying is that the good question contains a part of the answer. In the case of the challenge the findings depend heavily on the quality of the prepared data. It should be mentioned though that the flaws in the data preparation could lead to interesting discoveries as well.

In this particular challenge the problem was to discriminate between similar languages. The organizers indicated the groups; figure 1 presents them. The best way was to analyze the accuracy on every group apart; this information was not provided for the final test. We present and discuss it on the base of the 10-fold cross-validation experiment that used the 260,000 training instances.

languages	bg	mk
bg	19996	3
mk	1	19997

Table 3: Confusion table for Bulgarian and Macedonian

As it is seen from the table, Bulgarian and Macedonian can be reliably distinguished due to several specific characters in Macedonian alphabet which are frequent enough to appear in any sentence despite of the similarity of these two languages in both in vocabulary and syntax. A couple of misclassified sentences were written in a special manner; here is an example: "При то-зи из-раз ве-че яс-но си про-ли-ча, как да-ма-та уми-ш-ле-но вмъ-к-ва ня-ка-къв ак-цент, с дру-ги ду-ми бъл-гар-с-ки-ят й ве-че та-ка убя-г-ва, та чак го фъ-ф-ли."

languages	bs	hr	sr
bs	16168	2637	1195
hr	2977	16797	226
sr	2118	403	17479

Table 4: Confusion table for Bosnian, Croatian and Serbian

The worst results were obtained for the group of Bosnian, Croatian and Serbian languages as they overlap significantly in vocabulary, syntax and morphology. Although they claimed to be different languages the differences were not so frequent and easily identified as in case of Bulgarian and Macedonian. The most overlapping were Bosnian and Croatian; 13% of Bosnian sentences were classified as Croatian and 15% of Croatian sentences were classified as Bosnian.

languages	es-AR	es-ES
es-AR	17547	2453
es-ES	1607	18391

Table 5: Confusion table for Argentinean Spanish and Peninsular Spanish

The two Spanish dialects discrimination results were better than for Slavic languages; 12% of Argentinean Spanish sentences were classified as Peninsular Spanish and 9% of Peninsular Spanish sentences were classified as Argentinean Spanish. The differences here were also not so frequent and in many sentences were no any specific feature to help the source detection.

languages	pt-BR	pt-PT
pt-BR	18440	1558
pt-PT	1978	18021

Table 6: Confusion table for Brazilian Portuguese and European Portuguese

The situation for Brazilian Portuguese and European Portuguese was similar; 8% of Brazilian Portuguese sentences were classified as European Portuguese and 11% of European Portuguese sentences were classified as Brazilian Portuguese.

languages	id	my
id	19905	93
my	177	19823

Table 7: Confusion table for Indonesian and Malay

The differences between Indonesian and Malay are much more frequent and easily learned by a statistical system; less than 1% of sentences were misclassified.

It should be noted that the instances written in unknown languages and marked as xx were classified almost perfectly. Only several sentences were classified as Spanish but they seemed to be the Spanish ones; for example: "El manifiesto del Consell de la Llengua empieza afirmando que la lengua catalana "constituye una fuente de igualdad de oportunidades y de cohesión social en Balears".

The discussion raised in the corpora list disputed the question: has the problem of language discrimination finally been solved? The answer is no. Probably, the question should be reformulated as follows: is it even possible to obtain 100% correct discrimination between the languages, especially similar ones? And the answer would be again no. Languages are a part of the constantly changing world, so they also tend to be highly dynamic. Some languages disappear, some appear, some split, and some merge due to linguistic researches or political changes. For example, while we were solving the discrimination task between Serbian and Croatian but many linguists consider Serbian and Croatian to be dialects of one language, not separate languages and refer to it as Serbo-Croatian. The paper by Xia et al., (2010) presented an example of the complexity of language discrimination tasks. They presented a table of language names for which they could not even find a standard language ID code. There were also "missing" and ambiguous language names; tables of 1-to-n split of languages. They pointed out that our knowledge of languages is always changing and expanding, which entails the need of annual revision of the language list.

A good example of all said above is Moldavian language, which has been declared the official language with the new Moldovan Cyrillic alphabet due to political changes (appearance of Moldavian Republic as a part of Soviet Union). The differentiation of Moldavian and Romanian languages was introduced in the context of the Soviet policy that emphasized the differences between Moldova and Romania. Its existence is officially denied now because the current Moldavian government declared Romanian language as the official one in the Republic of Moldova. As in many other cases the new language was not linguistically but purely politically motivated. The linguists don't even want to delve deeper into that matter because there are many conflicting interests - political, cultural and even financial.

The other, pure practical question is: do we really need to obtain 100 percent accuracy in this task? The answer is also no. If the languages are really close some sentences are impossible to detect reliably; they could be written in any of related language and any language tool adapted to one of these languages is able to analyze it satisfactory.

References

Baldwin, T., Lui, M. 2010. *Language identification: The long and the short of the matter* (2010) In Proc. HLT-NAACL.

Bobicev, V. 2006. *Text Classification Using Word-Based PPM Models*, *The Computer Science Journal of Moldova*, vol. 14, no. 2, pp. 183–201.

Bobicev, V. 2007 *Comparison of Word-based and Letter-based Text Classification*. RANLP V, Bulgaria, pp. 76–80.

Bratko A., Cormack G. V., Filipic B., Lynam T. R., Zupan B. 2006. *Spam filtering using statistical data compression models*, Journal of Machine Learning Research 7:2673–2698.

Ljubešić, N., Kranjčić, D. 2014. *Discriminating between VERY similar languages among Twitter users.* 9th Language Technologies Conference Information Society – IS.

Malmasi, S. 2015. *Discriminating Similar Languages: Persian and Dari.* Volume 3 of Tiny Transactions on Computer Science.

Shannon, C. E. 1948. *A Mathematical Theory of Communication.* The Bell System Technical Journal, vol. 27, pp. 379–423, 623–656.

Tan, L., Zampieri, M., Ljubešic, N., Tiedemann, J. 2014. *Merging Comparable Data Sources for the Discrimination of Similar Languages: The DSL Corpus Collection.* Proceedings of the 7th Workshop on Building and Using Comparable Corpora (BUCC), Iceland.

Teahan, W. 1998. *Modelling English text*, PhD Thesis, University of Waikato, New Zealand.

Tetreault, J., Blanchard, D., Cahill, A. 2013. *A report on the first native language identification shared task.* In Proceedings of the Eighth Workshop on Innovative Use of NLP for Building Educational Applications, Atlanta, GA, USA. Association for Computational Linguistics.

Xia, F., Lewis, C., Lewis, W. D. 2010. *The Problems of Language Identification within Hugely Multilingual Data Sets,* Proceedings of the 7th International Conference on Language Resources and Evaluation (LREC 2010).

Zampieri, M., Tan, L., Ljubešić, N., Tiedemann, J. 2014. *A Report on the DSL Shared Task 2014.* 1st Workshop on Applying NLP Tools to Similar Languages, Varieties and Dialects (VarDial), Ireland.

Comparing Approaches to the Identification of Similar Languages

Marcos Zampieri[1,2], Binyam Gebrekidan Gebre[3], Hernani Costa[4] and Josef van Genabith[1,2]
Saarland University, Germany[1]
German Research Center for Artificial Intelligence (DFKI), Germany[2]
Max Planck Computing and Data Facility, Germany[3]
University of Malaga, Spain[4]

Abstract

This paper describes the submission made by the MMS team to the Discriminating between Similar Languages (DSL) shared task 2015. We participated in the closed submission track using only the dataset provided by the shared task organisers which contained short texts from 13 similar languages and language varieties. We submitted three runs using different systems and compare their performance. As a result, our best system achieved 95.24% accuracy for test set A (containing original texts) and 92.78% accuracy for test set B (containing texts without named entities).

1 Introduction

Automatic language identification is an important task in Natural Language Processing (NLP), which consists of applying computational methods to identify the language a document is written in. Language identification is often modelled as a classification task and it is often the first processing stage of many NLP applications and pipelines. Although language identification is largely considered to be a solved task, recent studies have shown that language identification systems often fail to achieve satisfactory performance across different datasets and domains (Lui and Baldwin, 2011), particularly with: datasets containing short pieces of texts such as *tweets* (Zubiaga et al., 2014); code-switching data (Solorio et al., 2014); or when discriminating between very similar languages (Zampieri et al., 2014).

Given these challenges, the Discriminating between Similar Languages (DSL) shared task provides an excellent opportunity for researchers interested in evaluating and comparing their systems' performance on discriminating between similar languages and language varieties using short text excerpts extracted from journalistic texts. For this purpose, the MMS[1] team developed three systems for the closed submission track of the DSL shared task 2015. The systems are explained in more detail in Section 4.

The remainder of the paper is structured as follows. First, Section 2 presents the most relevant approaches in the field. The DSL shared task 2015 is described in detail in Section 3. Then, our approach and the results obtained are presented in Sections 4 and 5 Finally, Section 6 presents the final remarks and highlights our future plans for improving the systems.

2 Related Work

There have been a number of papers published about the identification or discrimination of similar languages in recent years. Most of them use supervised classification algorithms and words and characters as features to solve the task. Unlike general-purpose language identification, most of the systems trained to discriminate between similar languages perform best using high order character n-grams and word n-gram representations.

Different groups or pairs of similar languages and language varieties have been studied using data from different sources such as standard contemporary newspapers and social media. Recent studies include: Indian languages (Murthy and Kumar, 2006), Malay and Indonesian (Ranaivo-Malançon, 2006), Mainland, Singapore and Taiwanese Chinese (Huang and Lee, 2008), Brazilian and European Portuguese (Zampieri and Gebre, 2012), South Slavic languages (Tiedemann

[1]MMS is an acronym for our affiliations/locations (Malaga, Munich and Saarland). In the shared task report (Zampieri et al., 2015) the team is displayed as MMS*. The * indicates that a shared task organiser is a team member.

Proceedings of the Joint Workshop on Language Technology for Closely Related Languages, Varieties and Dialects, pages 66–72,
Hissar, Bulgaria, September 10, 2015.

and Ljubešić, 2012; Ljubešić and Kranjčić, 2015) English varieties (Lui and Cook, 2013), Spanish varieties (Zampieri et al., 2013; Maier and Gómez-Rodrıguez, 2014), and Persian and Dari (Malmasi and Dras, 2015).

Over the last few years there has been a significant increase of interest in the computational processing of Arabic. This is evidenced by a number of research papers on different NLP tasks and applications including the identification/discrimination of Arabic dialects (Elfardy and Diab, 2014; Zaidan and Callison-Burch, 2014; Tillmann et al., 2014; Sadat et al., 2014; Salloum et al., 2014; Malmasi et al., 2015). From a purely engineering perspective, discriminating between dialects poses the same challenges as the discrimination between similar languages and language varieties.

3 The DSL Task

The shared task organisers provided all participants with an updated version of the DSL corpus collection v.2.0 (DSLCC) (Tan et al., 2014). This corpus is composed of 14 classes, 13 languages[2] and one class containing documents written in previously 'unseen' languages to emulate a real-world language identification scenario. Table 1 presents the languages included in the DSLCC v.2.0 corpus grouped by similarity.

Language/ Variety	Code
Bosnian	*bs*
Croatian	*hr*
Serbian	*sr*
Indonesian	*id*
Malay	*my*
Czech	*cz*
Slovak	*sk*
Brazilian Portuguese	*pt-BR*
European Portuguese	*pt-PT*
Argentine Spanish	*es-AR*
Castilian Spanish	*es-ES*
Macedonian	*bg*
Bulgarian	*mk*
Unknown	*xx*

Table 1: DSL corpus by language and variety.

In detail, the corpus collection contains 308,000 short text excerpts sampled from journalistic texts (22,000 per class) varying between 20 and 100 tokens per excerpt.

It is important to mention that these 22,000 texts per class are divided into 3 partitions, i.e. 18,000, 2,000 and 2,000 instances for training, development and testing, respectively. The test set is further subdivided into two test sets (A and B), each one containing 1,000 instances. While the test set A contains original texts, the organisers replaced named entities for place holders in the set B in order to decrease thematic bias in the classification process. Below we present an example of a Portuguese instance containing place holders *#NE#* instead of the named entities.

(1) Compara #NE# este sistema às indulgências vendidas pelo #NE# na #NE# #NE# quando os fiéis compravam a redenção das suas almas dando dinheiro aos padres.

Regarding the choice of only participating in the closed submission track, we first analysed the results of the 2014 edition where we realised that only two teams decided to participate in both open and closed submission tracks, namely UMich (King et al., 2014) and UniMelb-NLP (Lui et al., 2014). Both of them had better performance in the closed submission track and reported that more training data does not necessarily lead to higher performance and that the features learned by the classifiers are, to a certain extent, dataset specific. Therefore, we decided to use only the dataset provided by the organisers and only participate in the closed submission track.

4 Approach

Given that each team was allowed to submit a maximum of three runs to each track (closed and open), we decided to take this opportunity to test and compare different approaches. To do that, we developed three systems based on team MMS-member's previous work in language identification and related tasks. The first two systems were previously used for the Native Language Identification (NLI) (Gebre et al., 2013) and the third one has been applied to language variety identification. The following is a list of the three systems and the their corresponding submission runs:

- **Run 1** - Logistic Regression with TF-IDF Weighting

[2]For the sake of simplicity, we refer to both languages and language varieties as languages.

- **Run 2** - SVM with TF-IDF Weighting
- **Run 3** - Likelihood Estimation

It is important to mention that in each run we used different groups of features, all of them based on n-grams. In detail, for *Run 1* and *Run 2* we used n-grams ranging from bi- to seven-grams and 5-grams for *Run 3*.

4.1 TF-IDF Weighting

Term Frequency - Inverse Document Frequency (TF-IDF)[3] weighting measure was used in the systems developed for *Run 1* and *Run 2*.

Term Frequency refers to the number of times a particular term appears in a text.[4] It seems intuitive to think that a term that occurs more frequently tends to be a better identifier for the text than a term that occurs less frequently, however, this intuition does not take into account the relationship between the frequency of a term and its importance to the text. For this reason, we computed a logarithmic relationship (sublinear TF scaling) (Manning et al., 2008):

$$wf_{t,d} = \begin{cases} 1 + \log(tf_{t,d}) & \text{if } tf_{t,d} > 0 \\ 0 & \text{otherwise} \end{cases} \quad (1)$$

where $wf_{t,e}$ refers to weight and $tf_{t,e}$ refers to the frequency of term t in document d.

The $wf_{t,d}$ weight represents the importance of a term in a document based on its frequency. However, not all terms that occur frequently in a text are equally important for our purpose. As an example, lets suppose we need to train a classifier to distinguish between British and American English varieties. Words like *the, of, and* will be very frequent, but they are not discriminative, mostly because they are frequent in both varieties. On the other hand, words like *London* or *rubbish* might not be as frequent as *the, of, and*, yet, they are better discriminative words for British English. Therefore, the actual importance of a term for this task depends on how infrequent the term is in other texts. This can be modelled using Inverse Document Frequency (IDF). IDF is based on the assumption that a term which occurs in many texts is not a good discriminator, and should be given less weight than one which occurs in fewer texts. To summarize, IDF is the *log* of the inverse probability of a term being found in any document (Salton and McGill, 1986):

$$idf(t_i) = \log \frac{N}{n_i} \quad (2)$$

where N is the number of documents in the corpus, and term t_i occurs in n_i of them.

TF gives more weight to a frequent term in a document whereas IDF decreases this weight if the term occurs in many documents. On their own, these measures are not very powerful as when combined together to form the well-known TF-IDF measure. The TF-IDF formula combines the weights of TF and IDF by multiplying them. Returning to our example, *the* is a frequent English word so its TF value will be high, however, it is a frequent word in all English texts, in turn making its IDF value low.

Equation 3 shows the final weight that each term in a document gets before normalisation.

$$w_{i,d} = (1 + \log(tf_{t,d})) \times \log \frac{N}{n_i} \quad (3)$$

The texts included in the shared task dataset have different lengths ranging between 20 and 100 tokens each. To cope with this variation we normalised each document feature vector to unit length so that document length does not severely impact term weights. The resulting document feature vectors are fed into two different classifiers, Logistic Regression and SVM.

4.2 Classifiers

Systems developed for *Run 1* and *Run 2* were previously used in the Native Language Identification (NLI) (Gebre et al., 2013) shared task 2013 (Tetreault et al., 2013) by the Cologne-Nijmegen team with good results. They both rely on the TF-IDF weighting scheme combined with two different classifiers.

For *Run 1*, we opt for Logistic Regression using the LIBLINEAR open source library (Fan et al., 2008) from scikit-learn (Pedregosa et al., 2011) and fix the regularisation parameter to 100.0. This regression algorithm has been used in different classification problems including for example temporal text classification (Niculae et al., 2014).

[3] The TF-IDF description presented in this section is based on our previous work (Gebre et al., 2013)

[4] In our experiments, terms are n-grams of characters, words, part-of-speech tags or any combination of them.

For *Run 2*, we used a Support Vector Machine classifier (Joachims, 1998). This approach delivered a slightly better performance than Logistic Regression during the NLI shared task. On a very challenging dataset containing TOEFL essays written by speakers of 11 different languages, TF-IDF with SVM reached 81.4% and 84.6% accuracy on the test set when using 10-fold cross validation.

Finally, for *Run 3* we use a simple, yet efficient and fast method that combines Laplace smoothing and a probabilistic classifier. The approach was previously applied to distinguish Brazilian and European Portuguese texts (Zampieri and Gebre, 2012) and it is available as an open source tool called *VarClass* (Zampieri and Gebre, 2014). The likelihood function is calculated as described in equation 1.

$$P(L|text) = \arg\max_{L} \sum_{i=1}^{N} \log P(n_i|L) + \log P(L) \quad (4)$$

where N is the number of n-grams in the test text, n_i is the ith n-gram and L stands for the language models. Given a test text, we calculate the probability for each of the language models. The language model with the highest probability determines the identified language of the text.

5 Results

We start by reporting the official shared task results in terms of accuracy. Table 2 highlights the best results for each dataset.

Run	Test Set A	Test Set B
Run 1	94.09%	**92.77%**
Run 2	**95.24%**	**92.77%**
Run 3	94.07%	92.47%
Rank	2nd *out of 9*	4th *out of 7*

Table 2: Overall accuracy.

Results obtained by the three systems are very similar. Nevertheless, the SVM with TF-IDF Weighting approach obtained slightly better overall performance (*Run 2*). As we expected, the systems' performance drops from test set A to test set B. This means that our systems rely on named entities to discriminate between similar languages. It is important to point out that we did not do any specific training with the blinded named entities. Probably we could have achieved better results if we had prepared our systems to cope with this variation.

Table 3 presents the accuracy obtained by our best system (SVM with TF-IDF Weighting - *Run 2*) for each of the 14 classes. The results show that our best system achieved perfect performance in two of the language groups (Czech/ Slovak and Bulgarian/ Macedonian), probably due to exclusive characters present in one of the languages, as well as in identifying the 'unseen' languages in test set A.

Language/Variety	Test Set A	Test Set B
Bosnian	83.5%	76.6%
Croatian	91.8%	92.2%
Serbian	93.9%	90.7%
Indonesian	99.2%	97.5%
Malay	99.4%	99.5%
Czech	100%	99.9%
Slovak	100%	100%
Brazilian Portuguese	93.6%	90.5%
European Portuguese	93.0%	86.7%
Argentine Spanish	91.2%	89.2%
Castilian Spanish	94.8%	94.5%
Macedonian	100%	100%
Bulgarian	100%	100%
Unknown	100%	99.8%

Table 3: *Run 2*: performance per language.

Although the performance did not drop for Croatian and Malay when comparing test set A and B as it did for the rest of the languages, we do not think that this reflects any property of Croatian nor Malay nor any characteristics of the dataset. This is a simple preference of the classifier when distinguishing Croatian from Bosnian and Serbian, and Malay from Indonesian.

Tables 4, 5 and 6 present the confusion matrices obtained by the three systems using the 2,000 gold test instances.

Table 6 shows that Likelihood Estimation used for *Run 3* achieved higher scores when discriminating between language varieties, by classifying 1,912 Peninsular Spanish texts and 1,867 Brazilian Portuguese texts correctly. On the other hand, it was the only method which did not score 100% when classifying 'unseen' languages. Due to its simplicity, this method is well suited to discriminate between language varieties, hence the good results obtained in binary classification for Portuguese (Zampieri and Gebre, 2012), but

	bg	bs	cz	es-AR	es-ES	hr	id	mk	my	pt-BR	pt-PT	sk	sr	xx
bg	2000	0	0	0	0	0	0	0	0	0	0	0	0	0
bs	0	1578	0	0	0	241	0	0	0	0	0	0	181	0
cz	0	0	2000	0	0	0	0	0	0	0	0	0	0	0
es-AR	0	0	0	1774	226	0	0	0	0	0	0	0	0	0
es-ES	0	0	0	227	1773	0	0	0	0	0	0	0	0	0
hr	0	132	0	0	0	1841	0	0	0	0	0	0	26	1
id	0	0	0	0	0	0	1979	0	21	0	0	0	0	0
mk	0	0	0	0	0	0	0	2000	0	0	0	0	0	0
my	0	0	0	0	0	0	30	0	1970	0	0	0	0	0
pt-BR	0	0	0	0	0	0	0	0	0	1826	174	0	0	0
pt-PT	0	0	0	0	0	0	0	0	0	222	1778	0	0	0
sk	0	0	0	0	0	0	0	0	0	0	0	2000	0	0
sr	0	86	0	0	0	41	0	0	0	0	0	0	1873	0
xx	0	0	0	0	0	0	0	0	0	0	0	0	0	2000

Table 4: Confusion Matrix *Run 1* - Axis Y represents the actual classes and Axis X the predicted classes.

	bg	bs	cz	es-AR	es-ES	hr	id	mk	my	pt-BR	pt-PT	sk	sr	xx
bg	2000	0	0	0	0	0	0	0	0	0	0	0	0	0
bs	0	1661	0	0	0	193	0	0	0	0	0	0	146	0
cz	0	0	2000	0	0	0	0	0	0	0	0	0	0	0
es-AR	0	0	0	1796	204	0	0	0	0	0	0	0	0	0
es-ES	0	0	0	209	1791	0	0	0	0	0	0	0	0	0
hr	0	135	0	0	0	1843	0	0	0	0	0	0	21	1
id	0	0	0	0	0	0	1988	0	12	0	0	0	0	0
mk	0	0	0	0	0	0	0	2000	0	0	0	0	0	0
my	0	0	0	0	0	0	19	0	1981	0	0	0	0	0
pt-BR	0	0	0	0	0	0	0	0	0	1844	156	0	0	0
pt-PT	0	0	0	0	0	0	0	0	0	166	1834	0	0	0
sk	0	0	1	0	0	0	0	0	0	0	0	1999	0	0
sr	0	86	0	0	0	41	0	0	0	0	0	0	1891	0
xx	0	0	0	0	0	0	0	0	0	0	0	0	0	2000

Table 5: Confusion Matrix *Run 2* - Axis Y represents the actual classes and Axis X the predicted classes.

	bg	bs	cz	es-AR	es-ES	hr	id	mk	my	pt-BR	pt-PT	sk	sr	xx
bg	2000	0	0	0	0	0	0	0	0	0	0	0	0	0
bs	0	1623	0	0	0	198	0	0	0	0	0	0	179	0
cz	0	0	2000	0	0	0	0	0	0	0	0	0	0	0
es-AR	0	0	0	1623	377	0	0	0	0	0	0	0	0	0
es-ES	0	0	0	88	1912	0	0	0	0	0	0	0	0	0
hr	0	205	0	0	0	1746	0	0	0	0	0	0	49	0
id	0	0	0	0	0	0	1980	0	20	0	0	0	0	0
mk	0	0	0	0	0	0	0	2000	0	0	0	0	0	0
my	0	0	0	0	0	0	8	0	1992	0	0	0	0	0
pt-BR	0	0	0	0	0	0	0	0	0	1867	133	0	0	0
pt-PT	0	0	0	0	0	0	0	0	0	236	1764	0	0	0
sk	0	0	0	0	0	0	0	0	0	0	0	2000	0	0
sr	0	107	0	0	0	36	0	0	0	0	0	0	1857	0
xx	5	2	0	5	7	3	0	0	0	0	0	0	2	1976

Table 6: Confusion Matrix *Run 3* - Axis Y represents the actual classes and Axis X the predicted classes.

it clearly does not cope well with unseen data. Consequently, this method can be considered a good choice for situations in which all classes are known *a priori*.

6 Conclusion

This paper presented the MMS entry to the Discriminating between Similar Languages (DSL) shared task. We submitted three different approaches to deal with the task in hand, and their overall scores turned out to be very similar. The linear SVM classifier combined with TF-IDF weighting (*Run 2*) achieved slightly better results than the other two methods, i.e. 95.24% against 94.07% and 94.09% accuracy on test set A. The system ranked 2nd (out of 9 teams) on the test set A and 4th (out of 7 teams) on the test set B.

Based on the results, we observed that the systems' performance drop from test set A to test set B. This was already expected because named entities play an important role in this kind of task. One of the ways to cope with the influence of named entities in text classification is to use delexicalised text representations relying on POS tags or hybrid representations mixing word forms and grammatical categories. In our previous work, however, the results obtained using POS tags to discriminate between Spanish varieties, indicate that the use of more abstract text representations do not result in performance gain (Zampieri et al., 2013). In future work we would like to return to the question of text representation and investigate whether we can propose features that deliver high performance across multiple datasets.

An interesting approach would be to model these three systems hierarchically. This would result in a two-level classification task, first identifying the language group (grouped by similarity) and then the language itself. This approach was proposed by the NRC team, the DSL winner of the 2014 edition (Goutte et al., 2014). In the future we plan to investigate whether performing classification on two levels would increase the overall score or not.

Acknowledgements

Hernani Costa is supported by the People Programme (Marie Curie Actions) of the European Union's Framework Programme (FP7/2007-2013) under REA grant agreement n° 317471.

References

Heba Elfardy and Mona T Diab. 2014. Sentence level dialect identification in Arabic. In *Proceedings of ACL*.

Rong-En Fan, Kai-Wei Chang, Cho-Jui Hsieh, Xiang-Rui Wang, and Chih-Jen Lin. 2008. LIBLINEAR: A library for large linear classification. *Journal of Machine Learning Research*, 9:1871–1874.

Binyam Gebrekidan Gebre, Marcos Zampieri, Peter Wittenburg, and Tom Heskens. 2013. Improving native language identification with tf-idf weighting. In *Proceedings of the 8th BEA workshop*, Atlanta, USA.

Cyril Goutte, Serge Léger, and Marine Carpuat. 2014. The NRC system for discriminating similar languages. In *Proceedings of the VarDial Workshop*, Dublin, Ireland.

Chu-ren Huang and Lung-hao Lee. 2008. Contrastive approach towards text source classification based on top-bag-of-word similarity. In *Proceedings of PACLIC*, pages 404–410.

Thorsten Joachims. 1998. Text categorization with support vector machines: Learning with many relevant features. In *Proceedings of the European Conference on Machine Learning (ECML)*, pages 137–142. Springer.

Ben King, Dragomir Radev, and Steven Abney. 2014. Experiments in sentence language identification with groups of similar languages. In *Proceedings of the VarDial Workshop*, Dublin, Ireland.

Nikola Ljubešić and Denis Kranjčić. 2015. Discriminating between closely related languages on twitter. *Informatica*, 39(1).

Marco Lui and Timothy Baldwin. 2011. Cross-domain feature selection for language identification. In *Proceedings of 5th International Joint Conference on Natural Language Processing*, pages 553–561, Chiang Mai, Thailand, November. Asian Federation of Natural Language Processing.

Marco Lui and Paul Cook. 2013. Classifying English documents by national dialect. In *Proceedings of Australasian Language Technology Workshop*, pages 5–15.

Marco Lui, Ned Letcher, Oliver Adams, Long Duong, Paul Cook, and Timothy Baldwin. 2014. Exploring methods and resources for discriminating similar languages. In *Proceedings of VarDial*.

Wolfgang Maier and Carlos Gómez-Rodrıguez. 2014. Language variety identification in Spanish tweets. In *Proceedings of the LT4CloseLang Workshop*.

Shervin Malmasi and Mark Dras. 2015. Automatic Language Identification for Persian and Dari texts. In *Proceedings of PACLING 2015*, pages 59–64.

Shervin Malmasi, Eshrag Refaee, and Mark Dras. 2015. Arabic Dialect Identification using a Parallel Multidialectal Corpus. In *Proceedings of PACLING 2015*, pages 209–217, Bali, Indonesia, May.

Christopher D Manning, Prabhakar Raghavan, and Hinrich Schütze. 2008. *Introduction to information retrieval*. Cambridge University Press.

Kavi Narayana Murthy and G Bharadwaja Kumar. 2006. Language identification from small text samples. *Journal of Quantitative Linguistics*, 13(01):57–80.

Vlad Niculae, Marcos Zampieri, Liviu P Dinu, and Alina Maria Ciobanu. 2014. Temporal text ranking and automatic dating of texts. In *Proceedings of EACL*. ACL.

Fabian Pedregosa, Gaël Varoquaux, Alexandre Gramfort, Vincent Michel, Bertrand Thirion, Olivier Grisel, Mathieu Blondel, Peter Prettenhofer, Ron Weiss, Vincent Dubourg, et al. 2011. Scikit-learn: Machine learning in python. *The Journal of Machine Learning Research*, 12:2825–2830.

Bali Ranaivo-Malançon. 2006. Automatic identification of close languages - case study: Malay and Indonesian. *ECTI Transactions on Computer and Information Technology*, 2:126–134.

Fatiha Sadat, Farnazeh Kazemi, and Atefeh Farzindar. 2014. Automatic identification of Arabic language varieties and dialects in social media. In *Proceedings of SocialNLP 2014*.

Wael Salloum, Heba Elfardy, Linda Alamir-Salloum, Nizar Habash, and Mona Diab. 2014. Sentence level dialect identification for machine translation system selection. In *Proceedings of ACL*, pages 772–778, Baltimore, USA.

Gerard Salton and Michael J McGill. 1986. *Introduction to modern information retrieval*. McGraw-Hill, Inc.

Thamar Solorio, Elizabeth Blair, Suraj Maharjan, Steven Bethard, Mona Diab, Mahmoud Ghoneim, Abdelati Hawwari, Fahad AlGhamdi, Julia Hirschberg, Alison Chang, and Pascale Fung. 2014. Overview for the first shared task on language identification in code-switched data. In *Proceedings of the First Workshop on Computational Approaches to Code Switching*, pages 62–72, Doha, Qatar, October.

Liling Tan, Marcos Zampieri, Nikola Ljubešić, and Jörg Tiedemann. 2014. Merging comparable data sources for the discrimination of similar languages: The DSL corpus collection. In *Proceedings of The Workshop on Building and Using Comparable Corpora (BUCC)*, Reykjavik, Iceland.

Joel Tetreault, Daniel Blanchard, and Aoife Cahill. 2013. A report on the first native language identification shared task. In *Proceedings of BEA*, Atlanta, GA, USA, June.

Jörg Tiedemann and Nikola Ljubešić. 2012. Efficient discrimination between closely related languages. In *Proceedings of COLING 2012*, pages 2619–2634, Mumbai, India.

Christoph Tillmann, Saab Mansour, and Yaser Al-Onaizan. 2014. Improved sentence-level Arabic dialect classification. In *Proceedings of the VarDial Workshop*, pages 110–119, Dublin, Ireland, August.

Omar F Zaidan and Chris Callison-Burch. 2014. Arabic dialect identification. *Computational Linguistics*.

Marcos Zampieri and Binyam Gebrekidan Gebre. 2012. Automatic identification of language varieties: The case of Portuguese. In *Proceedings of KONVENS*, pages 233–237.

Marcos Zampieri and Binyam Gebrekidan Gebre. 2014. Varclass: An open source language identification tool for language varieties. In *Proceedings of Language Resources and Evaluation (LREC)*.

Marcos Zampieri, Binyam Gebrekidan Gebre, and Sascha Diwersy. 2013. N-gram language models and POS distribution for the identification of Spanish varieties. In *Proceedings of TALN*, pages 580–587.

Marcos Zampieri, Liling Tan, Nikola Ljubešić, and Jörg Tiedemann. 2014. A report on the DSL shared task 2014. In *Proceedings of the VarDial Workshop*, pages 58–67.

Marcos Zampieri, Liling Tan, Nikola Ljubešić, Jörg Tiedemann, and Preslav Nakov. 2015. Overview of the dsl shared task 2015. In *Proceedings of LT4VarDial*, Hissar, Bulgaria.

Arkaitz Zubiaga, Inaki San Vicente, Pablo Gamallo, José Ramom Pichel, Inaki Alegria, Nora Aranberri, Aitzol Ezeiza, and Víctor Fresno. 2014. Overview of tweetlid: Tweet language identification at sepln 2014. In *Proceedings of the Tweet Language Identification Workshop (TweetLID)*, Girona, Spain.

A two-level classifier for discriminating similar languages

Judit Ács
Budapest University of Technology and Economics
judit@aut.bme.hu

László Grad-Gyenge
Eötvös Loránd University
laszlo.grad-gyenge@creo.hu

Thiago Bruno Rodrigues de Rezende Oliveira
Universidade Federal do Vale do São Francisco
thiago_brro@hotmail.com

Abstract

The BRUniBP team's submission is presented for the Discriminating between Similar Languages Shared Task 2015. Our method is a two phase classifier that utilizes both character and word-level features. The evaluation shows 100% accuracy on language group identification and 93.66% accuracy on language identification. The main contribution of the paper is a memory-efficient correlation based feature selection method.

1 Introduction

The discrimination of similar languages (DSL) (Zampieri et al., 2015) can be defined as the subtask of the language identification (LI) problem. LI is a fundamental task in the area of natural language processing (NLP). The primary goal of LI is to determine the language of a written text. In practical applications, LI acts as a preprocessor of various NLP techniques as for example machine translation, sentiment analysis or even web search. LI is currently an actively researched topic, DSL is also in the focus of interest (Tiedemann and Ljubešić, 2012).

Unlike well-separated languages, multilingualism, varieties or dialects of language can seriously degrade the quality of LI. DSL, noisy data, non-well-formatted text, short sentences, mixed language (i.e. tweets) are other examples of challenging problems in this field. In this paper we focus on the DSL problem on a shared task. Our experiment shows that discrimination between Bosnian, Croatian and Serbian and between Argentinian and Peninsular Spanish are the most challenging tasks for our methods.

Most state of the art methods solve the DSL task in two phases. In the first phase the language group is to be identified, in the second phase the language is to be selected. The first decision of the model is more coarse and high level, the second labelling is to be more specialized as different language groups have different separating features. Regarding the information representation, most methods work with statistical features of the source text. The statistical features are n-grams at the word and at the character level. The parameter n in the fixed-length character and word n-gram models ranges from 1 to 6.

In our approach a maximum entropy classifier and SVM with different kernels were evaluated. The results show that maximum entropy delivers comparable results to SVM while it is considerably faster. To tackle the issue of zero probabilities resulting from unseen n-grams, Katz's back-off smoothing (Katz, 1987) is applied. Training a classifier on a large number of features requires substantial computing resources, which we do not have readily accessible. Features are pruned to less than 10,000 according to their pairwise Pearson correlation with the labels. The code is available on GitHub.[1]

Section 2 presents related work. Section 3 describes the dataset the methods are evaluated on. Section 4 provides an overview of the architecture of our method and describes the classification method. Section 5 gives insight into how the text is preprocessed before calculating the statistical features. Section 6 presents the evaluation results. Section 7 concludes the paper.

2 Related work

Most of the DSL methods have a two phase architecture. The first level is to determine the language group, the second level is to discriminate within the language group.

(Porta and Sancho, 2014) utilize maximum entropy models for the DSL task. The first classifier

[1] http://github.com/juditacs/dsl

Proceedings of the Joint Workshop on Language Technology for Closely Related Languages, Varieties and Dialects, pages 73–77,
Hissar, Bulgaria, September 10, 2015. ©2015 Association for Computational Linguistics

determines the language group, the second works with empirically selected features that achieved best performance for the specific language group. (Lui et al., 2014) also define a two phase approach involving a POS-tagger. (Goutte et al., 2014) label the language group with a probabilistic model based on word co-occurrences in documents. To discriminate at the language group level, SVM based classification is used. (King et al., 2014) compare naïve Bayes, logistic regression and SVM based classifiers. They also preprocess the data with manually defined methods as named entity removal and English word removal. (Purver, 2014) introduces a single-level approach, training a linear SVM on word and character n-grams of length 1-3.

3 Dataset

Our method is evaluated on the DSLCC dataset (Tan et al., 2014), which dataset is provided for the shared task. As Tan et al. describe the collection and the preparation of the dataset in detail, we only provide a summary in Table 1. The dataset contains 6 language groups of closely related languages and dialects plus one group called *other*. The language groups are presented in the first column (`Group`) of the table. The second column (`Language`) identifies the language, the third column (`code`) contains a short identifier for each language.

For each language, the dataset consists of 20 000 sentences. Each list of sentences is divided into two parts as 18 000 sentence training sample and 2 000 sentence development sample.

Group	Language	Code
A	Bulgarian	bg
	Macedonian	mk
B	Bosnian	bs
	Croatian	hr
	Serbian	sr
C	Czech	cs
	Slovak	sk
D	Argentinian Spanish	es-AR
	Peninsular Spanish	es-ES
E	Brazilian Portuguese	pt-BR
	European Portuguese	pt-PT
F	Malay	my
	Indonesian	id
X	other	xx

Table 1: Language groups and languages

4 Method

To solve the shared task, we introduce a two-level architecture. On the first level we utilize a classifier to distinguish between the language groups. We refer to this classifier later as *inter-group classifier*. The inter-group classifier is described in Section 4.1. To conduct a more specialized decision, to distinguish between the languages in a language group, a second-level classifier is utilized. This classifier is titled the *intra-group* classifier and is described in Section 4.2

4.1 Inter-group classifier

Although the dataset contains 7 language groups, we trained the classifier on 14 labels according to the languages (instead of groups) and grouped the corresponding labels together according to the language groups.

From the variety of features tested (see Section 4.2), tf-idf delivered the best results for the inter-group classification. Although tf-idf is a more common method for information retrieval tasks, it can also be defined for the current task as follows

document set of all sentences in one language,

term one word, see Section 5 for details,

query one test sentence.

The inter-group classifier operates in two steps. In the first step the top 100,000 keywords are extracted for each language. In the second step the weighted sum of keywords is computed for each sentence in each language and the language with the highest score is chosen.

The inter-group classifier provides 100% accuracy on language group identification. Regarding language labelling, the accuracy of the inter-group classifier is 92.54%.

We used the following tf, idf and qf weightings:

$$tf_{t,d} = \log(1 + f_{t,d}),$$

where $f_{t,d}$ is the raw frequency of a term in all sentences in a language.

$$idf_t = \log(1 + \frac{N}{n_t}),$$

where N is the number of languages and n_t is the number of languages in which term t appears and

$$qf_t = \left(0.5 + 0.5\frac{f_{t,q}}{\max_t f_{t,q}}\right) \times \log\frac{N}{n_t},$$

where qf_t is the weight of term t, $\max_t f_{t,q}$ is the highest *tf* score for term t in any language.

4.2 Intra-group classifier

The language groups are refined by the intra-group classifier further. In the case of groups A, C, D, E and F, there are 2 languages two distinguish between. In the case of group B, there are 3 languages to label. In the case of "group" X there is only 1 language, the intra-group classifier is not used in this case.

Various features are extracted and 6 models are trained for the 6 groups. Character and word n-grams, Katz's backoff scores, tf-idf scores and stopword n-grams are used as features.

4.2.1 N-grams

Character n-grams proved to be the most prominent feature in last year's DSL task (Zampieri et al., 2014). However, the number of character n-grams grows exponentially with n in theory and subexponentially in practice but it still results in a large number of features. This is the reason why we involved feature selection.

Since PCA and other popular dimension reduction methods are very memory-intensive, Pearson correlation is involved as a feature selection method. To select the most relevant features, for each feature, the absolute value of the Pearson correlation with the labels is calculated and based on this value, the top n features are selected.

4.2.2 Katz's backoff smoothing

Our baseline system is an implementation of Katz's backoff smoothing with training option that works well in the general setting.[2] It is possible to train and test with this system up to $n = 4$ grams with reasonable memory consumption. For further memory-saving, see Section 5.

There are several variants of Katz's backoff smoothing, the one used here discounts the Maximum Likelihood estimations with a constant factor and distributes the leftover probability mass according to lower order n-grams.

$$P_{bo}(c_n|c_1,\ldots,c_n) = \\ = \begin{cases} \frac{C(c_1,\ldots,c_n)-d}{C(c_1,\ldots,c_{n-1})}, & \text{if } C(c_1,\ldots,c_n) > 0 \\ \alpha_{c_1,\ldots,c_{n-1}} P_{bo}(c_n|c_2,\ldots,c_{n-1}) & \text{otherwise,} \end{cases}$$

where $\alpha_{c_1,\ldots,c_{n-1}}$ is the left-over probability mass from discounting:

$$\alpha_{c_1,\ldots,c_{n-1}} = 1 - \sum_{c_n : C(c_1,\ldots,c_n)>0} \frac{C(c_1,\ldots,c_n) - d}{C(c_1,\ldots,c_{n-1})}.$$

The probabilities for all the languages are calculated on n-grams of various size, n is ranging from 1 to 4. The language with the highest probability is selected. Both the probabilities and the language are used as features and are passed to the intra-group classifier.

4.2.3 Tf-idf

Similarly to the case of the inter-group classifier, tf-idf scores are calculated for each language group. The language group specific tf-idf scores are based on the sentences only in the specific language group. The tf-idf scores are the used as features later for the intra-group classification.

4.2.4 Word bigrams

Word bigrams are extracted and after selection are used as features. The selection of word bigrams is similar to the selection of the character n-grams. The absolute value of Pearson correlation of the bigrams with the labels is calculated and then the top n bigrams are selected. In our experiment n is set to 1 000.

4.2.5 Stopwords

Although language varieties may use virtually the same vocabulary, we assume that common expressions, word and clause order may differ and the order of stopwords reflects this difference. In each language, we filtered the corpus to its 200 most frequent words, most of which are stopwords. The filtered sentences were fed as input to the tf-idf (see Section 4.1) and the word bigram extractor (see Section 4.2.4), resulting in a much smaller feature number, therefore no feature selection was necessary.

[2] `https://github.com/juditacs/langid`

	Accuracy
run1	0.9331428571
run2	0.9366428571
run3	0.9348571429

Table 2: Overall accuracy of our three runs

4.2.6 Classifier

Scikit-learn's (Pedregosa et al., 2011) maximum entropy and SVM based classifiers are evaluated. In the case of SVM, different kernels are utilized. Due to space limitations and focus we do not publish these evaluation results. As the maximum entropy classifier delivers comparable results to the SVM based method, we use the maximum entropy classifier as it is considerably faster.

5 Preprocessing and tokenization

In order to reduce the number of components that do not contribute much to language identification, the corpus is preprocessed before feature extraction. The preprocessing pipeline consists of the following steps

lowercasing Python's `unicode.lower` function is used

puncutation filtering standard punctuation (Python's `string.punctuation`) and additional quotation symbols are removed

whitespace normalization multiple consecutive whitespaces in the same sentence are replaced with a single space

digit replacement numbers are replaced with a single 0

All steps are applied before feature extraction except in the case of tf-idf, where lowercasing is not performed.

The preprocessed text is tokenized with NLTK (Bird, 2006). Although the tokenizer is trained on English punctuation corpus, it performs reasonably well for the current languages.

6 Results

Three runs are submitted. The first two runs are the same except that in the second run we took advantage of the fact that the labels were balanced. The third run only differed in thresholding for group B. The overall accuracy of each run is listed in Table 2 and the detailed results of our best run can be found in Table 3.

Group	Languages	Accuracy
A	bg,mk	1.0
B	bs,hr,sr	0.8417
C	cs,sk	1.0
D	es-AR,es-ES	0.867
E	pt-BR,pt-PT	0.929
F	id,my	0.998
other	xx	1.0
sum	0.9366	

Table 3: Detailed results of our best run

To have a deeper insight into the limitations of solving the shared task, a manual evaluation has been performed on the 152 sentences misclassified Portuguese sentences by our best run by two Brazilian native speakers. The annotators have been asked to label each sentence as BR (Brazilian), PT (European Portuguese) or UN (Unknown). UN tag has been introduced to avoid guessing. Their very low agreement on the labels (Cohen's kappa 0.28) and the fact that only 22 sentences have been labeled correctly (according to the gold standard) by both of them suggests that there is very little room for improvement on the shared task.

7 Conclusion

We presented the system description of our DSL2015 task submission which performed an overall accuracy of 93.66%. We ended up the 5th place out of 8 submissions.

We introduced a two-level classifier with a variety of features: character and word n-grams, tf-idf, stopword bigrams and tf-idf, and smoothed language models. The first level solely relies on the output of tf-idf, capable of grouping languages with 100% accuracy. The second level combines all features and uses the maximum entropy classifier to classify languages within language groups.

Memory efficiency is a key issue in our research. Our most important steps consume less than 5GB RAM.

References

Steven Bird. 2006. NLTK: the natural language toolkit. In *Proceedings of the COLING/ACL on Interactive presentation sessions*, pages 69–72. Association for Computational Linguistics.

Cyril Goutte, Serge Léger, and Marine Carpuat. 2014. The NRC system for discriminating similar languages. In *Proceedings of the First Workshop on Applying NLP Tools to Similar Languages, Varieties and Dialects*, pages 139–145, Dublin, Ireland, August. Association for Computational Linguistics.

S. Katz. 1987. Estimation of probabilities from sparse data for the language model component of a speech recognizer. *IEEE Transactions on Acoustics, Speech and Signal processing*, 35(3):400–401.

Ben King, Dragomir Radev, and Steven Abney. 2014. Experiments in sentence language identification with groups of similar languages. In *Proceedings of the First Workshop on Applying NLP Tools to Similar Languages, Varieties and Dialects*, pages 146–154, Dublin, Ireland, August. Association for Computational Linguistics.

Marco Lui, Ned Letcher, Oliver Adams, Long Duong, Paul Cook, and Timothy Baldwin. 2014. Exploring methods and resources for discriminating similar languages. In *Proceedings of the First Workshop on Applying NLP Tools to Similar Languages, Varieties and Dialects*, pages 129–138, Dublin, Ireland, August. Association for Computational Linguistics.

F. Pedregosa, G. Varoquaux, A. Gramfort, V. Michel, B. Thirion, O. Grisel, M. Blondel, P. Prettenhofer, R. Weiss, V. Dubourg, J. Vanderplas, A. Passos, D. Cournapeau, M. Brucher, M. Perrot, and E. Duchesnay. 2011. Scikit-learn: Machine learning in Python. *Journal of Machine Learning Research*, 12:2825–2830.

Jordi Porta and José-Luis Sancho. 2014. Using maximum entropy models to discriminate between similar languages and varieties. In *Proceedings of the First Workshop on Applying NLP Tools to Similar Languages, Varieties and Dialects*, pages 120–128, Dublin, Ireland, August. Association for Computational Linguistics.

Matthew Purver. 2014. A simple baseline for discriminating similar languages. In *Proceedings of the First Workshop on Applying NLP Tools to Similar Languages, Varieties and Dialects*, pages 155–160, Dublin, Ireland, August. Association for Computational Linguistics.

Liling Tan, Marcos Zampieri, Nikola Ljubešic, and Jörg Tiedemann. 2014. Merging comparable data sources for the discrimination of similar languages: The dsl corpus collection. In *Proceedings of the 7th Workshop on Building and Using Comparable Corpora*, pages 11–15, Reykjavik, Iceland.

Jörg Tiedemann and Nikola Ljubešić. 2012. Efficient discrimination between closely related languages. In *Proceedings of COLING 2012*, pages 2619–2634, Mumbai, India.

Marcos Zampieri, Liling Tan, Nikola Ljubešić, and Jörg Tiedemann. 2014. A report on the DSL Shared Task 2014. In *Proceedings of the First Workshop on Applying NLP Tools to Similar Languages, Varieties and Dialects*, pages 58–67, Dublin, Ireland, August. Association for Computational Linguistics.

Marcos Zampieri, Liling Tan, Nikola Ljubešić, Jörg Tiedemann, and Preslav Nakov. 2015. Overview of the DSL Shared Task 2015. In *Proceedings of the Joint Workshop on Language Technology for Closely Related Languages, Varieties and Dialects (LT4VarDial)*, Hissar, Bulgaria.

Experiments in Discriminating Similar Languages

Cyril Goutte, Serge Léger
Multilingual Text Processing
National Research Council Canada
Ottawa, ON K1A0R6
Firstname.Lastname@nrc.ca

Abstract

We describe the system built by the National Research Council (NRC) Canada for the 2015 shared task on *Discriminating between similar languages*. The NRC system uses various statistical classifiers trained on character and word ngram features. Predictions rely on a two-stage process: we first predict the language group, then discriminate between languages or variants within the group. This year, we focused on two issues: 1) the ngram generation process, and 2) the handling of the anonymized ("blinded") Named Entities. Despite the slightly harder experimental conditions this year, our systems achieved an average accuracy of 95.24% (closed task) and 95.65% (open task), ending up second or (close) third on the closed task, and first on the open task.

1 Introduction

Although language identification is largely considered a solved problem in the general setting, a number of frontier cases are still under study. For example, when little data is available (eg single twitter post), when the input is mixed or when discriminating similar languages or language variants.

The *Discriminating between similar languages* (DSL) shared task offers precisely such a situation, by offering an interesting mix of close languages and variants, and relatively short, one-sentence texts. This year, four groups contain similar languages:

- Bosnian, Croatian and Serbian;
- Indonesian and Malaysian;
- Czech and Slovakian;
- Bulgarian and Macedonian.

Two groups contain variants of the same language:

- Portuguese: European vs. Brazilian;
- Spanish: European vs. Argentinian.

In addition, instances to classify are single sentences, a more realistic and challenging situation than full-document language identification.

There are two interesting additions to the 2015 challenge. A second test set, with Named Entity anonymized, was added to evaluate the influence of local information on the predictions. In addition, sentences from "other", unknown languages were added to the test sets. This means that group/language prediction is not limited to the 13 languages in the training set.

Following some good results at last year's evaluation (Goutte et al., 2014; Zampieri et al., 2014), we took part to this years evaluation in order to see how our system would handle the additional language pair, and the two challenges of anonymized named entities and more varied test data. In addition, we wanted to further explore the way character ngrams should be more efficiently extracted from the raw text.

The overall longer term motivation is to use language and variant detection to help natural language processing, for example in machine translation (Zbib et al., 2012). Discriminating similar languages may also be a first step to identify code switching in short messages (Elfardy et al., 2013).

The following section describes the models we used, and the features we extracted from the data. We then briefly describe the data we trained on (Section 3), and summarize our experimental results in Section 4.

2 Models

Our approach relies on a two-stage process. We first predict the language group, then discriminate the languages or variants (which for convenience

Proceedings of the Joint Workshop on Language Technology for Closely Related Languages, Varieties and Dialects, pages 78–84,
Hissar, Bulgaria, September 10, 2015.

we simply all call "language" from now on) within the group. This approach works best if the first stage (i.e. group) classifier has high accuracy, because if the wrong group is predicted, it is impossible to recover from that mistake in the second stage. On the other hand, as most groups only comprise two languages, our two-stage process makes it possible to rely on a simple binary classifier within each group, and avoid the extra complexity that comes with multiclass modeling.

We first describe the features we extract from the data (Section 2.1). We then provide a quick overview of how the probabilistic group classifier works (Section 2.2). Finally, we describe the within-group language predictors in Section 2.3.

2.1 Features

Based on previous experience, we focus on character and word ngrams as features. We generate several feature spaces, depending on the basic sequence unit (character or word), size of the ngram (N) and way to extract it from the sentence to classify.

bowN: Within-sentence consecutive subsequence of N words. We focus on unigrams (bag of words) and bigrams, as higher orders seem to degrade performance. Bigrams use special tokens to mark begining and end of sentences.

charN: Character ngrams, extracted from the complete sentence including whitespaces and punctuation.

pcharN: Character ngrams, extracted from the complete sentence including whitespaces, but removing the punctuation.

scharN: Within-word character ngrams, after removing punctuation. Word boundaries are included, but ngrams are not extracted over two or more words. Words smaller than the ngram size are include, e.g. "I" yields the ngram "_I_" for $N \geq 3$.

For character ngrams, we generated all feature spaces corresponding to $N = 2 \dots 6$, while we limit word ngrams to `bow1` and `bow2`. We index all ngrams observed at least once in the entire collection.

2.2 Group Prediction

Predicting the language group, including **X**, is a 7-way classification task. For this first stage, we use the same probabilistic model as last year (Gaussier et al., 2002; Goutte et al., 2014). This model offers a convenient and fast way to handle the group prediction, and its performance on last years' data proved excellent. This is a generative model for co-occurrences of words w in documents d. It models the probability of co-occurrence $P(w, d)$ as a mixture model over classes c:

$$P(w, d) = P(d) \sum_{c} P(w|c)P(c|d), \qquad (1)$$

where $P(w|c)$ is the profile for class c, ie the probability that each word[1] w in the vocabulary may be generated for class c, and $P(c|d)$ is the profile for document d, ie the probability that a word from that document is generated from each class. This is a supervised version of the *Probabilistic Latent Semantic Analysis* model (Hofmann, 1999), similar to *Naïve Bayes* (McCallum and Nigam, 1998), except that instead of sampling the class once per document and generating all words from that class, this model can resample the class for each word in the document. This results in a much more flexible model, and higher performance.

Model estimation is done by maximum likelihood and is identical to *Naïve Bayes*:

$$\widehat{P}(w|c) = \frac{1}{|c|} \sum_{d \in c} n(w, d). \qquad (2)$$

Model behaviour depends solely on this set of class profile vectors. They provide lexical probabilities for each class. For predicting class assignment for a new document, we introduce the new document $\widetilde{d}$ and associated, unknown parameters $P(\widetilde{d})$ and $P(c|\widetilde{d})$. We estimate the posterior assignment probability $P(c|\widetilde{d})$ by *folding in* $\widetilde{d}$ into the collection and maximizing the log-likelihood of the new document,

$$\widetilde{\mathcal{L}} = \sum_{w} n(w, \widetilde{d}) \log P(\widetilde{d}) \sum_{c} P(c|\widetilde{d})P(w|c),$$

with respect to $P(c|\widetilde{d})$, keeping the class profiles $P(w|c)$ fixed. This is a convex optimization problem that may be efficiently solved using the iterative Expectation Maximization algorithm (Demp-

[1] In the context of this study, a "word" w is a (word or character) *ngram*, according to Section 2.1.

ster et al., 1977). The resulting iterative, fixed-point equation is:

$$P(c|\widetilde{d}) \leftarrow P(c|\widetilde{d}) \sum_{w} \frac{n(w,\widetilde{d})}{|\widetilde{d}|} \frac{P(w|c)}{\sum_c P(c|\widetilde{d})P(w|c)}, \quad (3)$$

where $|\widetilde{d}| = \sum_w n(w,\widetilde{d})$ is the length of document $\widetilde{d}$. Because the minimization is convex w.r.t. $P(c|\widetilde{d})$, the EM update converges to the unique maximum.

Given a corpus of annotated documents, model parameters are estimated using Eq. 2. This is extremely fast and ideal for training on the large corpus available for this evaluation. At test time, we initialize $P(c|\widetilde{d})$ with the uniform distribution and run the EM equation (3) until convergence for each test sentence. Although this phase is slower than training, it may be easily and efficiently parallelized on, e.g. multicore architecture.

Note that the 7-way group prediction task is, in practice, handled using a 14-class model predicting the languages (including "Other"), and mapping the predictions to the 7 groups.

2.3 Language Prediction

Once the group is predicted from the previous stage, within-group language prediction becomes a binary classification problem in most groups, or a 3-way classification problem in group **A**.

For groups B to G, we rely on Support Vector Machines, powerful binary discriminative classifiers which typically perform very well on text. In our experiments, we use the SVM_{light} (Joachims, 1998) implementation. We trained a binary SVM on each of the feature spaces described in Section 2.1. The training examples are limited to the two languages within the group under consideration. Each SVM is therefore trained on a smaller document set, making training more manageable. We used a linear kernel, and set the C parameter in SVM_{light} to the default value. Prediction with a linear kernel is very fast as it only requires computing the dot product of the vector space representation of a document with the equivalent linear weight vector for the model.

For group A, we need to handle the 3-way multiclass situation to discriminate between Bosnian, Croatian and Serbian. This is done by first training one linear SVM per class in a one-versus-all fashion. We then apply a calibration step using a Gaussian mixture on SVM prediction scores in order to transform these scores into proper posterior probabilities (Bennett, 2003). We then predict the class with the highest calibrated probability. Once the calibration model has been estimated on a small held-out set, applying the calibration to the three models and picking the highest value is very efficient.

2.4 Voting

Each feature space (Section 2.1) yields a set of group and language classifiers. Each may yield different performance and make different mistakes. There are several ways to combine different feature sets.

One method is to concatenate features into a larger, single feature space on which classifiers are trained. Choosing the feature spaces to combine and concatenating them poses some (mild) computational and combinatorial problems. In addition, we did not find this approach particularly effective in our 2014 experiments, so we did not consider it this year.

Another approach is to combine outputs from models trained on different feature spaces. This can be done by training a combination model using these outputs as its inputs, as in, e.g., stacked generalization (Wolpert, 1992). Of course, this requires training an additional model, setting aside data to estimate it, etc. Previous investigations (Goutte et al., 2013) suggest that a simpler approach is actually more effective. We simply combine the output of models by voting: for a given set of models trained on different feature spaces, each model votes for the class it predicts, and the final prediction goes to the class with the most votes. In order to simplify the choice of the set of models, we rank all feature spaces according to their cross-validated prediction error, and pick the number of models that yields the highest performing vote, again according to cross-validation. This simple approach is surprisingly and consistently effective. One explanation is that prediction errors for different models tend to be *independent*, so that these errors usually don't conspire towards the wrong prediction.

3 Data

For the **closed task** experiments, we used the DSLCC v.2.0 corpus provided by the organizers (Zampieri et al., 2015). This corpus covers 13 languages in 6 groups, plus "Other". Although the number of groups and languages is similar to last year's shared task (Zampieri et al., 2014), the English group was dropped in favour of a new group for Bulgarian and Macedonian, called **G** in Table 1. For the closed task experiment, no other resource of any sort was used.

For the **open task**, we combined the DSLCC v.2.0 data used for the closed task with the relevant portion of the DSLCC v.1.0 provided last year (Tan et al., 2014). Specifically, we ignore the two variants of English from the 2014 collection, and added the rest to the 2015 training data. We actually tried to use the DSLCC v.2.1 collection, with the additional Mexican Spanish and Macanese Portuguese data, to check whether this would help improve the group prediction (first stage), but that did not help according to the cross-validation estimator.

Note that the data is nicely balanced across classes. We used a stratified 10-fold cross-validation estimator, respecting the class proportions across folds, in order to estimate prediction performance. The data provided as *development* set was used as one fold in this estimator.

Table 1 shows the size of the training and test sets. Two test sets were provided: test set A contains original unmodified sentences, while test set B was modified to replace named entities with a placeholder (`#NE#`). Our closed task system used only the "Train 2015" data, while the open task added the "Train 2014" data to estimate models.

One key difference between the 2014 and 2015 data is the sentence length. In 2015, all sentences have between 20 and 100 words, while in 2014, they had up to 600 words in some groups.

4 Results

4.1 Submitted Systems

We ended up submitting two runs to each of the tasks (close and open), and each of the test sets (A and B), resulting in eight runs in total. The difference between the closed and open tasks runs is simply the data used for training, as explained in the previous section.

For test set A, our first run is the best system using a single feature space, as estimated by 10-fold cross-validation, Our second run is the best voting combination, again estimated by cross-validation.

For test set B, we focused on feature spaces that would be relatively insensitive to the anonymized named entity. We removed the `#NE#` placeholder in test set B before extracting the `bow1` and all `scharN` ngram features. Our first run is the best system using only character ngrams, which ends up being `schar6` in all cases. Our second run is trained on bag of words, `bow1`. No voting combination was used on test set B, resulting as expected in lower performance.

Task	closed				open			
Test set	A		B		A		B	
Run #	1	2	1	2	1	2	1	2
# errors	3	3	5	4	1	2	2	2

Table 2: Number of errors (out of 14000 test sentences) made by the group-level classifier for the eight runs (two runs per task and per test set).

4.2 Group Prediction

We first look at the number of mistakes made by the group-level predictor. As mentioned above, this is important because the language prediction further down the line will be unable to recover from mistakes made at the group level.

The number of group-level errors varies depending on the task (closed or open) and the feature space used (best or vote). On the closed task, the cross-validated accuracy is 99.971% for the best feature space (`pchar6`) and 99.976% for the best vote (`pchar6`, `bow1` and `char6`), corresponding to 80 and 67 errors, respectively, out of 280,000 examples. For the open task, the accuracy is 99.977% for the best and 99.979% for the vote, i.e. respectively 64 and 59 errors. Most of the errors are caused by **X** (Other) documents being predicted in the **E** (Spanish) group.

Table 2 shows the number of actual prediction errors made on the test sets by the group-level classifiers for each of our eight runs. Note that in last year's shared task, a single test document was incorrectly classified at the group level. This year shows a large increase, especially on test set B, for which we did not have any example document before the test phase. The open task, using more data, allows for slightly better performance.

4.3 Language Prediction

Tables 3 and 4 show all results obtained by our runs, as well as the results per group. The overall picture is similar to last year's evaluation. Group **A** is the hardest, followed by the Spanish (**E**) and Portuguese (**D**) varieties groups. Groups **B** and

Group	Language or Variety	# sentences Train 2015	Train 2014	Test sets A	B
	Bosnian	20,000	20,000	1000	1000
A	Croatian	20,000	20,000	1000	1000
	Serbian	20,000	20,000	1000	1000
B	Indonesian	20,000	20,000	1000	1000
	Malaysian	20,000	20,000	1000	1000
C	Czech	20,000	20,000	1000	1000
	Slovak	20,000	20,000	1000	1000
D	Brazil Portuguese	20,000	20,000	1000	1000
	Portugal Portuguese	20,000	20,000	1000	1000
E	Argentine Spanish	20,000	20,000	1000	1000
	Spain Spanish	20,000	20,000	1000	1000
G	Bulgarian	20,000	-	1000	1000
	Macedonian	20,000	-	1000	1000
X	Others ("xx")	20,000	-	1000	1000

Table 1: Number of sentences in the Discriminating Similar Languages Corpus Collections (DSLCC) provided for the 2014 and 2015 shared tasks, plus test sets with (A) or without (B) named entities, across groups and languages. The system for the closed task was trained on 2015 data only, the system for the open task was trained on 2014 and 2015 data.

Task	closed							
Test set	A				B			
Run #	1		2		1		2	
	Acc.	#err	Acc.	#err	Acc.	#err	Acc.	#err
Group A	88.53	344	89.90	303	87.00	390	84.57	463
Group B	99.30	14	99.35	13	98.80	24	98.90	22
Group C	99.95	1	99.95	1	100.0	0	99.95	1
Group D	92.40	152	92.70	146	86.75	265	86.15	277
Group E	89.40	212	89.95	201	85.20	296	84.35	313
Group G	99.95	1	99.95	1	100.0	0	100.0	0
Overall	94.82	725	**95.24**	666	**93.01**	979	92.30	1078

Table 3: Language prediction test accuracy for the **closed task**, both test sets and all runs. Our best results are in bold (tied for second overall). Overall #err is larger than column sum due to "Other".

Task	open							
Test set	A				B			
Run #	1		2		1		2	
	Acc.	#err	Acc.	#err	Acc.	#err	Acc.	#err
Group A	89.90	303	90.43	287	87.47	376	85.87	424
Group B	99.50	10	99.60	8	98.65	27	98.85	23
Group C	99.95	1	100.0	0	100.0	0	100.0	0
Group D	92.90	142	93.05	139	87.85	243	87.35	253
Group E	90.90	182	91.35	173	86.30	274	85.35	293
Group G	99.95	1	99.95	1	100.0	0	100.0	0
Overall	95.43	640	**95.65**	609	**93.41**	922	92.89	995

Table 4: Language prediction test accuracy for the **open task**, both test sets and all runs. Our best results are in bold (first overall). Overall #err is larger than column sum due to "Other".

especially **C** and **G** are relatively easy, reaching above 99% performance.

Performance is clearly impacted by removing the named entities, as shown by the results on test set B. This degrades the accuracy by around 2%. This clearly shows that named entities help language detection. In our case, this effect is somewhat amplified by the fact that we did not run a voting system on test set B. As shown by the test set A results, voting brings us 0.25-0.5% improvements in accuracy. On the other hand, it is slightly surprising that on the two groups with highest performance (**C** and **G**), we get perfect performance on test set B while we make one mistake on test set A. Of course this could be due to sample variation, as test set A and B are different.

In last year's evaluation (Zampieri et al., 2014), two groups (Lui et al., 2014; King et al., 2014) compiled additional textual material in several languages in order to compete in the open track. Their submission on the open track turned out several points of accuracy *lower* than their performance on the closed track. By contrast, our inclusion of the DSLCC v.1.0 from last year in our open submission helped us consistently reduce the number of errors by about 10% (a boost of at least 0.4% in accuracy). This may be due to the fact that despite the differences in sentence length, DSLCC v.1.0 was fairly similar to this year's corpus, and helped more than independently acquired material. This is a typical domain adaptation effect, often observed in natural language processing.

We also note that the final test accuracy on test set A was very well estimated by the 10-fold cross-validation, always with 0.5% and typically much less.

5 Conclusions

We described the National Research Council's entry to the second shared task on *Discriminating between similar languages*. Our system uses a fairly straightforward processing and modeling approach, building a two stage predictor relying on a probabilistic document classifier to predict the group, and Support Vector Machines to identify the language within each group. We tested various word and character ngram features. Group-level classification was very accurate, making only a handful of mistakes mostly due to the presence of confounding documents from other languages. Our top system yields an average accuracy of 95.65% on test set A (open task), the top result (by a hair) reported on this new collection. Performance on test set B is clearly impacted by the lack of named entities, degrading average accuracy by about 2%. On the closed task, accuracy is 0.4% lower

Acknowledgments

This work was partly supported by the National Research Council programs Multimedia Analytic Tools for Security (MATS) and Learning and Performance Support Systems (LPSS).

References

Paul N. Bennett. 2003. Using asymmetric distributions to improve text classifier probability estimates. In *Proceedings of the 26th Annual International ACM SIGIR Conference on Research and Development in Informaion Retrieval*, SIGIR '03, pages 111–118, New York, NY, USA. ACM.

A. P. Dempster, N. M. Laird, and D. B. Rubin. 1977. Maximum likelihood from incomplete data via the EM algorithm. *Journal of the Royal Statistical Society, Series B*, 39(1):1–38.

Heba Elfardy, Mohamed Al-Badrashiny, and Mona Diab. 2013. Code switch point detection in arabic. In *18th International Conference on Applications of Natural Language to Information Systems*, pages 412–416.

Éric Gaussier, Cyril Goutte, Kris Popat, and Francine Chen. 2002. A hierarchical model for clustering and categorising documents. In *Proceedings of the 24th BCS-IRSG European Colloquium on IR Research: Advances in Information Retrieval*, pages 229–247, London, UK, UK. Springer-Verlag.

Cyril Goutte, Serge Léger, and Marine Carpuat. 2013. Feature space selection and combination for native language identification. In *Proceedings of the Eighth Workshop on Innovative Use of NLP for Building Educational Applications*, pages 96–100, Atlanta, Georgia, June. Association for Computational Linguistics.

Cyril Goutte, Serge Léger, and Marine Carpuat. 2014. The NRC system for discriminating similar languages. In *Proceedings of the 1st Workshop on Applying NLP Tools to Similar Languages, Varieties and Dialects (VarDial)*, Dublin, Ireland.

Thomas Hofmann. 1999. Probabilistic latent semantic analysis. In *Proc. of Uncertainty in Artificial Intelligence, UAI'99*, pages 289–296.

Thorsten Joachims. 1998. Text categorization with Suport Vector Machines: Learning with many relevant features. In Claire Nédellec and Céline Rouveirol, editors, *Proceedings of ECML-98, 10th European Conference on Machine Learning*, volume 1398 of *Lecture Notes in Computer Science*, pages 137–142. Springer.

Ben King, Dragomir Radev, and Steven Abney. 2014. Experiments in sentence language identification with groups of similar languages. In *Proceedings of the 1st Workshop on Applying NLP Tools to Similar Languages, Varieties and Dialects (VarDial)*, Dublin, Ireland.

Marco Lui, Ned Letcher, Oliver Adams, Long Duong, Paul Cook, and Timothy Baldwin. 2014. Exploring methods and resources for discriminating similar languages. In *Proceedings of the 1st Workshop on Applying NLP Tools to Similar Languages, Varieties and Dialects (VarDial)*, Dublin, Ireland.

Andrew McCallum and Kamal Nigam. 1998. A comparison of event models for Naive Bayes text classification. In *AAAI-98 Workshop on Learning for Text Categorization*, pages 41–48. AAAI Press.

Liling Tan, Marcos Zampieri, Nikola Ljubešić, and Jörg Tiedemann. 2014. Merging comparable data sources for the discrimination of similar languages: The DSL corpus collection. In *Proceedings of the 7th Workshop on Building and Using Comparable Corpora (BUCC)*, Reykjavik, Iceland.

David H. Wolpert. 1992. Stacked generalization. *Neural Networks*, 5:241–259.

Marcos Zampieri, Liling Tan, Nikola Ljubešić, and Jörg Tiedemann. 2014. A report on the DSL shared task 2014. In *Proceedings of the 1st Workshop on Applying NLP Tools to Similar Languages, Varieties and Dialects (VarDial)*.

Marcos Zampieri, Liling Tan, Nikola Ljubešić, Jörg Tiedemann, and Preslav Nakov. 2015. Overview of the DSL shared task 2015. In *Proceedings of the Joint Workshop on Language Technology for Closely Related Languages, Varieties and Dialects (LT4VarDial)*, Hissar, Bulgaria.

Rabih Zbib, Erika Malchiodi, Jacob Devlin, David Stallard, Spyros Matsoukas, Richard Schwartz, John Makhoul, Omar F. Zaidan, and Chris Callison-Burch. 2012. Machine translation of arabic dialects. In *Proceedings of the 2012 Conference of the North American Chapter of the Association for Computational Linguistics: Human Language Technologies*, pages 49–59, Montréal, Canada, June. Association for Computational Linguistics.

Building Monolingual Word Alignment Corpus for the Greater China Region

Fan Xu, Xiongfei Xu, Mingwen Wang*, Maoxi Li
School of Computer Information Engineering, Jiangxi Normal University
Nanchang 330022, China
{xufan,mwwang,mosesli}@jxnu.edu.cn, xuxiongfei1989@sina.com

Abstract

For a single semantic meaning, various linguistic expressions exist the Mainland China, Hong Kong and Taiwan variety of Mandarin Chinese, a.k.a., the Greater China Region (GCR). Differing from the current bilingual word alignment corpus, in this paper, we have constructed two monolingual GCR corpora. One is a 11,623-triple GCR word dictionary corpora which is automatically extracted and manually annotated from 30 million sentence pairs from Wikipedia. The other one is a manually annotated 12,000 sentence pairs GCR word alignment corpus from Wikipedia and news website. In addition, we present a rule-based word alignment model which systematically explores the different word alignment case, e.g. 1-1, 1-n and m-n mapping, from Mainland China to Hong Kong or Taiwan. Evaluation results on our two different GCR word alignment corpora verify the effectiveness of our model, which significantly outperforms the current Hidden Markov Model (HMM) based method, GIZA++ and their enhanced versions.

1 Introduction

There are different expressions for a single concept among the Mainland China, Hong Kong and Taiwan variety of Mandarin Chinese. For example, "信息/*xin xi*/information" and "分词/*fen ci*/word segmentation" are the valid expressions in Mainland China, while "资讯/*zi xun*/information", and "断词/*duan ci*/word segmentation" are the corresponding expressions in Chinese Hong Kong and Taiwan, respectively. Although these expressions are different, they have the same semantic meanings.

Generally, the automatic word alignment task is to find word-level translation correspondences in the parallel text or sentences. In specific, given a source sentence e consisting of words $e_1, e_2, \ldots, e_l$ and a target sentence f consisting of words $f_1, f_2, \ldots, f_m$, one needs to infer an alignment a, a sequence of indices $a_1, a_2, \ldots, a_m$ corresponding to source words e_{a_i} or a null word. Automatic word alignment plays a critical role in statistical machine translation.

Basically, the source sentence and the target sentence are usually written in different languages in the conventional word alignment corpora. Therefore, most current word alignment models are designed for bilingual word alignment corpus, such as Chinese-English (Ayan and Dorr, 2006), Japanese-English (Takezawa et al., 2002) and French-English (Mihalcea and Pedersen, 2003). However, little work focuses on the word alignment only in one language but with different script, e.g. Mandarin with simplified and traditional scripts, or different Mandarin dialects.

Motivated by the above observation, we have constructed two GCR corpora in this work. One is a 11,623-triple GCR word dictionary corpus which is automatically extracted and manually annotated from 30 million sentence pairs from Wikipedia. The other one is a manually annotated 12,000 sentence pairs GCR word alignment corpora obtained from Wikipedia and news website, respectively. Furthermore, we present a rule-based word alignment model which systematically explores the different word alignment case, e.g. 1-1, 1-n, and m-n mapping, from Chinese Mainland to Hong Kong or Taiwan. Evaluation results on our GCR word alignment corpora verify the effectiveness of our model, which significantly outperforms the current HMM based method, GIZA++ and their enhanced versions.

* Corresponding author

Proceedings of the Joint Workshop on Language Technology for Closely Related Languages, Varieties and Dialects, pages 85–94, Hissar, Bulgaria, September 10, 2015.

Actually, our corpora may be used as a linguistic resources to test whether automatic mining of Mandarin words across different regions. Or, it may be used as a resource to transliterate between simplified and traditional variant of Mandarin, like a tool offered by ICU (International Components for Unicode)[2].

The rest of this paper is organized as follows. Section 2 overviews the related work. In Section 3, we describe the annotation framework and scheme. Section 4 illustrates the annotation and statistics of the GCR triples (word dictionary) corpus. Section 5 presents the annotation of our GCR word alignment corpus, along with a rule-based word alignment model. In Section 6, we evaluate our model and the current representative word alignment models on the two corpora, and we conclude this work in Section 7 and present future directions.

2 Related Work

In this section, we list the representative word alignment corpus and word alignment computational models.

2.1 Word Alignment Corpus

In the past decade, several word alignment corpora between different languages have been proposed, e.g. Chinese-English (Ayan and Dorr, 2006), Japanese-English (Takezawa et al., 2002) and French-English (Mihalcea and Pedersen, 2003). They are annotated either at word-level or phrase-level alignment between two different languages. However, few researchers pay attention to the word alignment only in one language with different script, e.g. Mandarin with simplified and traditional scripts, or different Mandarin dialects. This is the motivation of our work.

2.2 Word Alignment Computational Model

To address the bilingual word alignment problem, many representative word alignment models based on machine learning technology have been designed so far. These models could be roughly divided into two categories, i.e., the generative models and the discriminative models.

To be more specific, IBM Model 1 (Brown et al., 1993) and Hidden Markov Model (HMM) (Vogel et al., 1996) are two generative word alignment modes where the word alignment probability is represented using Equation (1).

$$P(f|e)=\sum_{a}(\prod_{j=1}^{J} p_d(a_j \mid a_{j-})p_t(f_j \mid e_{a_j})) \quad (1)$$

where $e=\{e_1,...,e_I\}$ is a source sentence and $f=\{f_1,...,f_J\}$ is a target sentence; $a=\{a_1,...,a_J\}$ is an alignment vector such that $a_j=i$ indicates the j-th target word aligns to the i-th source word; j_- is the index of the last non null-aligned target word before the index j. The difference between the IBM model 1 and HMM model is that for the distortion probability $p_d(a_j=i|a_{j-}=i')$ is uniform in the IBM model 1 while proportional to the relative count $c(i-i')$ in the HMM model. Since then, a great amount of modified methods have been proposed to improve the distortion probability or the lexical translation probability (Och and Ney, 2003; DeNero and Macherey, 2011; Neubig et al., 2011; Kondo et al., 2013; Chang et al., 2014; Songyot and Chiang, 2014).

In contrast, many discriminative models have also been presented, such as those work proposed by Tamura et al. (2014), Yang et al. (2013), Blunsom and Cohn (2006), Moore (2005), Taskar et al. (2005). In particular, for a sentence pair (e, f), they seek the solution of Equation (2).

$$\bar{a} = \arg\max_a \sum_{i=1}^{n} \lambda_i f_i(a, e, f) \quad (2)$$

where $\bar{a}$ is the alignment, f_i are features and the λ_i are their weights.

3 GCR Word Alignment Framework and Scheme

In this section, we describe the annotation framework and the annotation scheme including elementary annotation unit identification and annotation training for the different GCR triples (word dictionary) and word alignment corpus.

3.1 Annotation Framework

Figure 1 shows the annotation framework. We choose Wikipedia and parallel news website as the different data source. The motivation is twofold:

(1)Wikipedia includes the same parallel texts written in simplified script for Chinese Mainland, and traditional script for Chinese Hong Kong and Taiwan simultaneously. Therefore we can extract GCR word dictionary/triples corpus.

(2)We can verify our word alignment computational model on the two different word alignment

[2] http://www.icu-project.org/

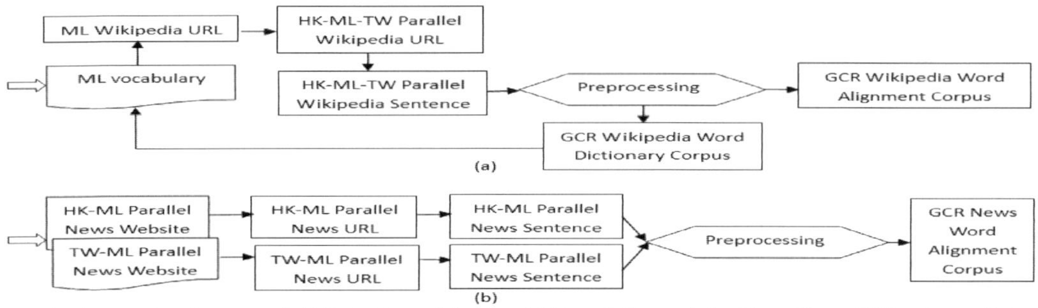

Figure 1: Annotation framework (ML indicates Mainland China, HK stands for Hong Kong, TW refers to Taiwan)

corpora from Wikipedia and news website.

The whole process in Figure 1 includes the parallel Wikipedia or news URL and sentence generation, followed by preprocessing phase and corpus generation phase. As shown in Figure (1.a), we select the initial ML(Mainland China) vocabulary[3](about 50,000 words) and HK(Hong Kong)-ML or TW(Taiwan)-ML parallel news website[4] as our data source. The preprocessing phase illustrated in Figure 1 includes sentence boundary detection, word segmentation, part-of-speech and name entity recognition (the name of people, or the name of locations, or the name of organizations).

In specific, we firstly adopt the jsoup[5] utility to iteratively crawl the parallel texts written in simplified script for Chinese Mainland and traditional script for Hong Kong and Taiwan from the Wikipedia.

Secondly, we take punctuations of "." or "!" or "?" or ";" as the sentence boundary, and employ ICTCLAS[6] and Ikanalyzer[7] to generate word segmentatio and part-of-speech and name entity identification for the sentence. Then, we generate parallel sentence pairs written in simplified script for Chinese Mainland and sentences written in traditional script for Hong Kong and Taiwan, respectively.

Thirdly, the parallel sentence pairs are used to generate the GCR triples (word dictionary) corpus and word alignment corpora.

We set two tasks for post processing the corpora. In task 1, word dictionary extraction, one only needs to extract the partial sentence after removing the longest common substrings written in simplified script for Chinese mainland and traditional script for the Chinese Hong Kong and Taiwan. In the second task, i.e., word alignment, one needs to annotate the whole sentence in the parallel sentence pairs. We solve the above two tasks independently because that the word alignment task is time-consuming. If we extract the different word of sequence from the annotated word alignment corpus, the size of the word dictionary will be very small.

3.2 Annotation Scheme

In this section, we address the key issues with the GCR triples (word dictionary) and word alignment annotation, such as Elementary Annotation Unit (EAU) identification and annotation training.

3.2.1 Elementary Annotation Unit

In linguistics, a morpheme is the smallest grammatical unit and the smallest meaningful unit of a language. Due to the difficulty of recognizing morpheme in a sentence, we adopt the word segmentation unit and name entity unit as the EAU.

3.2.2 Annotation Training

Our annotator team consists of a Ph.D. in Mandarin linguistics as the supervisor (senior annotator) and two graduate students in Mandarin linguistics as annotators (junior annotator). The annotation is done in three phases. In the first phase, the annotators learn the annotation scheme, especially word segmentation, name entity identification, along with the use of the word alignment annotation tool[8] (we revised the annotation tool according to our task). In the second phase, the two junior annotators annotate the same parallel sentence pairs independently. In the final phase, the senior annotator carefully proofreads all the final word alignment corpora.

[3] http://pinyin.sogou.com/dict/detail/index/2441
[4] http://www.takungpao.com/ and http://www.taiwan.cn/
[5] http://jsoup.org/
[6] http://ictclas.nlpir.org/
[7] https://github.com/blueshen/ik-analyzer
[8] https://github.com/desilinguist/wordalignui

4 GCR Word Dictionary Corpus

In this section, we address the key issues in the GCR word dictionary annotation, such as initial and final word dictionary generation.

4.1 Initial Word Dictionary Generation

In order to reduce human's workload and expand the size of the GRC word dictionary corpora, we firstly automatically generate the initial word dictionary represented as triples for the GCR, and then manually annotate the initial triples one by one. Figure 2 shows the detail algorithm.

Input: SS_{ML}, SS_{HK}, SS_{TW}
// SS_{ML}, SS_{HK}, SS_{TW} are the sentences set of Chinese Mainland, Hong Kong, and Taiwan, respectively.
Output: Triples[]
// Store the words of Chinese Mainland, Hong Kong, and Taiwan.

1. **BEGIN**
2. **For** each sentence s in SS_{ML}
3. slcs ← `LCS`(SS_{MLs}, SS_{HKs}, SS_{TWs})
4. **For** each word of sequence *ws* in slcs
5. $Section_{MLs}$ ← SS_{MLs} - *ws*;
6. $Section_{HKs}$ ← SS_{HKs} - *ws*;
7. $Section_{TWs}$ ← SS_{TWs} - *ws*;
8. **If**(#`Segment`($Section_{MLs}$)==#`Segment`($Section_{HKs}$)==#`Segment`($Section_{TWs}$))
9. Triples[] ← `push_back`(`Segment`($Section_{MLs}$, $Section_{HKs}$, $Section_{TWs}$))
10. **End If**
11. **End For**
12. **End For**
13. **Return** Triples[]
14. **End**

Figure 2: Initial GCR word dictionary generation algorithm

More specifically, we automatically extract about 1,853,136 web pages written in simplified script for Chinese Mainland and traditional script for Chinese Hong Kong and Taiwan, and generate 3,267,380 valid sentence pairs. After that, we generate initial triples using the above algorithm as shown in Figure 2, where function `LCS()` on Line 3 in Figure 2 stands for the Longest Common Subsequence (Václáv and David, 1975) in parallel sentence pairs written in simplified script for Chinese Mainland and traditional script for Hong Kong and Taiwan, Line 5-7 refer to the word of sequence after removing the longest common word subsequence, function `Segment()` on Line 8 indictates the word segmentation process for the section of the sentence after removing the LCS, function `push_back()` on Line 9 stands for adding the word segmentaion into the array *Triples[]*, Line 9 generates the triples if the size of the word segmentation are equal for each $Section_{MLs}$, $Section_{HKs}$ and $Section_{TWs}$.

In short, we firstly extract the LCS between the parallel sentences, then collect the different word of sequence, thirdly we segment the different portions, and finally generate the initial triple if the size of the segmentation of the different portions are same. Currently, we have generated 12,375 initial triples using the above algorithm as shown in Figure 2. To be more specific, column 2 in Table 1 illustrates the statistics of the initial GCR triples (word dictionary). We illustrate the algorithm using the example shown in Figure 3. After removing the longest common subsequence, we segment the remnant word of sequence, and get the "信息 /*xin xi*/information", "资讯/*zi xun*/information", "链接/*lian jie*/linking", and "连结/*lian jie*/connection" pairs accordingly. We take sentences written in simplified script for Chinese mainland as a bridge, and conduct similar process for sentence pairs for Chinese mainland and Taiwan. Then we can get the initial word dictionary (triples).

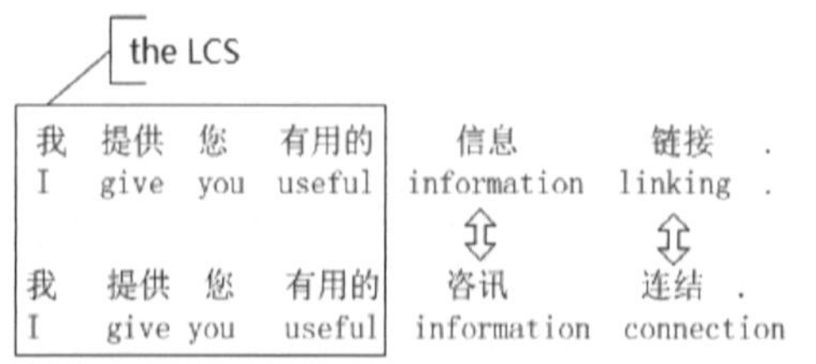

Figure 3: A parallel sentence pairs written in simplified script for Chinese mainland and traditional script for Hong Kong

4.2 Final Word Dictionary Generation

After generating the initial GCR triples (word dictionary), we conduct annotation training in Section 3.2.2 to generate final word dictionary.

Specifically, we let the two junior annotators on checking the feasibility of the same initial triples individually with the help of Google, Baidu and Wikipedia. Finally, the senior annotator carefully proofreads all the final triples presented by the two junior annotators.

Due to the difficulty of named entity annotation, we only annotate the availability of the triples with type of nouns, verbs, adjectives and others category (preposition, pronouns, connectives, quantifier). Finally, we get 11.623 triples, and list the statistics in column 3 of Table 1. According to Table 1, without considering the name entity, the type of nouns accounts for the greatest proportion, followed by the type of verbs, the type of others, and the type of adjectives. Besides, according to the accuracies reported in column 4, the initial triples are effective for type of nouns with 81.91% and type of verbs with 76.08%, respectively. This demonstrates the effectiveness of our initial GCR word dictionary generation algorithm under nouns and verbs cases.

Category	# of initial triples	# of final triples	accuracy
Nouns	2377	1947	0.8191
Verbs	715	544	0.7608
Adjectives	123	69	0.5610
Others (preposition, pronouns, connectives, quantifiers)	235	140	0.5957
the name of people	8280	8280	1.0
The name of locations	626	626	1.0
the name of organizations	17	17	1.0

Table 1: The statistics of the initial and final GCR triples

For clarity, Table 2 lists some specific GCR triples examples. Although the expression is different, they are semantically the same.

Chinese Mainland	Chinese Hong Kong	Chinese Taiwan
代码(Code)	程式码(Code)	程式码(Code)
出租车(Taxi)	的士(Taxi)	计程车 (Taxi)
官阶 (Official rank)	职衔 (Official rank)	职衔(Official rank)
查找(Find)	寻找(Find)	寻找(Find)
哈利姆(Halim)	哈林(Halim)	哈林(Halim)

Table 2: Some GCR word dictionary examples

Category	ML vs. HK(%)	ML vs. TW(%)	HK vs. TW(%)
Nouns	0.7543	0.8372	0.4998
Verbs	0.807	0.8699	0.3986
Adjectives	0.8455	0.8618	0.4634
Others	0.8213	0.8681	0.4340.
Initial Name Entity (the name of people)	0.8522	0.7022	0.6227
Initial Name Entity (The name of locations)	0.6278	0.893	0.6086
Initial Name Entity (the name of organizations)	0.7059	0.8235	0.6471

Table 3: The difference between Chinese Mainland, Hong Kong and Taiwan

Table 3 illustrates the difference between Chinese Mainland (ML for short), Hong Kong (HK for short), and Taiwan (TW for short) for the final GCR triples (word dictionary) in more details. According to the table, it is not surprising that the difference gap is remarkable between the Chinese Mainland and Hong Kong, also between the Chinese Mainland and Taiwan, while the difference gap is relatively smaller between Hong Kong and Taiwan. The reason is that Chinese Mainland use simplified script, while Hong Kong and Taiwan adopt traditional script.

5 GCR Word Alignment Corpus & Its Computational Model

Similar to Section 4, in this section, we address the key issues in the GCR word alignment annotation, such as tagging strategies, corpus quality, together with the statistics of the corpora.

5.1 Tagging Strategies

Firstly, we automatically extract 10,000 sentence pairs from Wikipedia (5,000 for Mainland-Hong Kong and 5,000 for Mainland-Taiwan) and 2,000 sentence pairs from news website (1,000 for Mainland-Hong Kong and 1,000 for Mainland-Taiwan) after the preprocessing phase described in Section 3.1. Then, we employ the word alignment annotation tool shown in Figure 4 to annotate word alignment for the GCR.

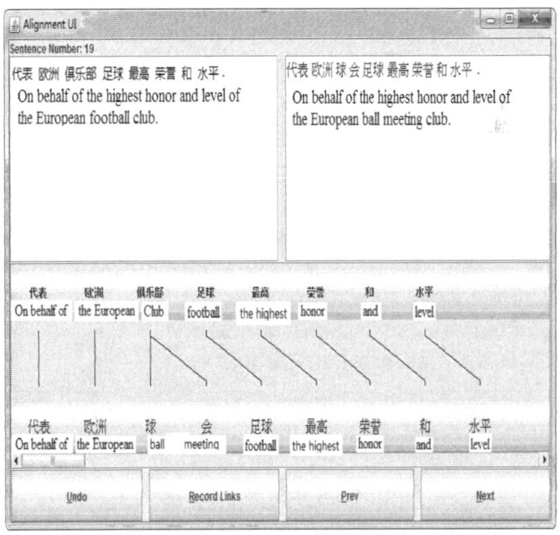

Figure 4: A GCR word alignment example

Figure 5 illustrates an example to show our annotation process for the parallel sentence pairs. The two junior annotators annotate the 12,000 parallel sentence pairs one by one independently. They need to annotate not only the same words of the pair but also the different ones. Finally, the senior annotator carefully proofreads all the final word alignment corpora.

Figure 5: An example is shown to extract the different word segment

5.2 Quality Assurance

We adopt the following two steps to ensure the quality of our GCR word alignments corpora.

Parallel Sentence Filtering. The more name entities exist in parallel sentence pairs, the more noisy is the final corpora. Therefore, we automatically filter out the sentence pairs containing more than one name entity accordingly.

Inter-annotator Consistency. Due to the lack of the size information of the word alignment in the parallel sentences, we cannot adopt Kappa measures to calculate the Inter-Annotator Agreement (IAA) in this work. To ensure the quality of our GCR word alignment corpora, we adopt the inter-annotator consistency using agreement on the whole 12,000 sentence pairs. We calculate the IAA using the division of the number of the same word alignments between the two annotators h1 and h2 by the total number of words in the sentence written in the Mainland Mandarin, showning in Equation (3).

$$IAA = \frac{\#\,\mathrm{wordAlignment}(h_1, h_2)}{\#\,\mathrm{words}(ML)} \quad (3)$$

Table 4 illustrates the inter-annotator consistency in details. As shown, the agreement on overall GCR word alignment corpora for both Chinese Mainland-Hong Kong and Chinese Mainland-Taiwan reaches above 94% and 97% for Wikipedia and news website, respectively. These justify the appropriateness of our corpus scheme, and guarantee the quality of the whole GCR word alignment corpora.

	IAA
Chinese Mainland vs. Hong Kong (Wikipedia)	0.9418
Chinese Mainland vs. Taiwan (Wikipedia)	0.9512
Chinese Mainland vs. Hong Kong (News Website)	0.9726
Chinese Mainland vs. Taiwan (News Website)	0.9754

Table 4: Inter-annotator consistency

5.3 Rule-based Word Alignment Computational Model

In this section, we present a 2-phase rule-based word alignment computational model.

Phase 1: **Different Parallel Word Segmentation Extraction**

Similar to the GCR initial triples generation process as shown in algorithm in Figure 2, we extract the different word segmentation between the parallel sentence pairs after removing the longest common subsequence. To be more specific, we show an example in Figure 5 to explain the whole process. As it is shown, we first extract two longest common subsequences, and then extract the different word segmentation after removing the two LCS. That is, we extract the different word segmentations as "俱乐部/*ju le bu*/Club" for the Chinese Mainland and "球 会/*qiu hui*/Boll meeting" for the Chinese Hong Kong accordingly.

Phase 2: **Word Alignment Mapping Rule**

After extracting the different word segmentations, we represent the word alignment model according to 3 cases, below, as shown in Table 5.

Case	Instance
1-1 mapping	文件 (file) — 档案 (archive)
1-n mapping	发达国家 (the developed country) — 已 开发 国家 (the developed country)
m-n mapping	大 萧条 (great depression) — 经济 大 恐慌 (great depression)

Table 5: A rule-based word alignment model

As it is shown, our rule-based word alignment model systematically explores the different word alignment case, e.g. 1-1, 1-n and m-n mapping, from Chinese Mainland to Hong Kong or Taiwan.

Specifically, 1-1 mapping indicates the number of the different word segmentation equals to 1 for ML, or HK, or TW; 1-n mapping stands for one of the number of the different word segmentation equals to 1, while the number of the different word segmentation equals to n for another; m-n

	Wikipedia Word Alignment Corpus			News Word Alignment Corpus		
Model	Precision	Recall	F1	Precision	Recall	F1
			Chinese Mainland vs. Hong Kong			
GIZA++(→)	0.8411	0.8684	0.8545	0.8792	0.8933	0.8862
GIZA++(←)	0.7247	0.7428	0.7335	0.7458	0.7496	0.7477
HMM	0.8020	0.8175	0.8097	0.8402	0.8437	0.8419
SYM_HMM	0.7859	0.7976	0.7917	0.8186	0.8193	0.8190
PIALIGN(→)	0.8701	0.8765	0.8733	0.8997	0.8824	0.8910
PIALIGN(←)	0.8694	0.8745	0.8720	0.8932	0.8714	0.8822
Moses_grow	0.9095	0.9043	**0.9069**	0.9254	0.9194	0.9224
Ours	0.9093	0.8750	0.8918	0.9465	0.9067	**0.9262**
			Chinese Mainland vs. Taiwan			
GIZA++(→)	0.8644	0.8927	0.8783	0.8986	0.9220	0.9102
GIZA++(←)	0.7259	0.7406	0.7332	0.7128	0.7256	0.7191
HMM	0.8094	0.8241	0.8167	0.8093	0.8180	0.8136
SYN_HMM	0.7948	0.8072	0.8009	0.7886	0.7971	0.7928
PIALIGN(→)	0.8854	0.8913	0.8883	0.8971	0.9061	0.9016
PIALIGN(←)	0.8866	0.8896	0.8881	0.8978	0.9004	0.8991
Moses_grow	0.9010	0.9012	**0.9011**	0.9165	0.9152	0.9158
Ours	0.9115	0.8708	0.8907	0.9419	0.9135	**0.9274**

Table 6: Precision, Recall and F1 scores of the different word segmentation pairs

	Wikipedia Word Alignment Corpus			News Word Alignment Corpus		
Model	Precision	Recall	F1	Precision	Recall	F1
			Chinese Mainland vs. Hong Kong			
GIZA++(→)	0.8373	0.8886	0.8622	0.8536	0.9017	0.8770
GIZA++(←)	0.7137	0.7475	0.7302	0.7183	0.7395	0.7288
HMM	0.7679	0.7686	0.7683	0.7549	0.7454	0.7454
SYN_HMM	0.7630	0.7569	0.7599	0.7603	0.7462	0.7532
PIALIGN(→)	0.8588	0.8985	0.8782	0.8738	0.8899	0.8818
PIALIGN(←)	0.8571	0.8974	0.8768	0.8589	0.8798	0.8692
Moses_grow	0.8847	0.9093	**0.8969**	0.8819	0.9055	0.8935
Ours	0.9093	0.8750	0.8918	0.9465	0.9067	**0.9262**
			Chinese Mainland vs. Taiwan			
GIZA++(→)	0.8586	0.9078	0.8825	0.8631	0.9198	0.8906
GIZA++(←)	0.7144	0.7462	0.7300	0.6830	0.7235	0.7027
HMM	0.7836	0.7872	0.7854	0.7498	0.7487	0.7493
SYM_HMM	0.7841	0.7803	0.7822	0.7518	0.7437	0.7477
PIALIGN(→)	0.8759	0.9056	0.8906	0.8556	0.9025	0.8784
PIALIGN(←)	0.8690	0.9032	0.8858	0.8549	0.9018	0.8777
Moses_grow	0.8964	0.9220	**0.9090**	0.8921	0.9130	0.9024
Ours	0.9115	0.8708	0.8907	0.9419	0.9135	**0.9274**

Table 7: Precision, Recall and F1 scores of the all sentence pairs

mapping refers to the case which is not belong to 1-1 mapping or 1-n mapping case.

6 Experimentation

In this section, we present the experiment settings including the benchmark datasets and baseline systems, and the experiment results for the different word segmentation pairs and the all sentence pairs accordingly.

6.1 Experiment Settings

Dataset. Currently, we take the proposed two different GCR word alignment corpora as our benchmark datasets.

Baselines. We choose several baseline methods. They are the Berkeley aligner utility[9] with HMM (Liang et al., 2006), SYN_HMM (DeNero and Klein, 2007), PIALIGN (Neubig et al., 2011),

[9] https://code.google.com/p/berkeleyaligner/

Model	Mapping Case	Precision	Recall	F1
GIZA++(→)	1-1 mapping	0.8678	0.9741	0.9179
	1-n mapping	0.8517	0.7345	0.7888
	m-n mapping	-	-	-
GIZA++(←)	1-1 mapping	0.7253	0.9835	0.8349
	1-n mapping	0.7432	0.1045	0.1832
	m-n mapping	-	-	-
HMM	1-1 mapping	0.8170	0.9779	0.8902
	1-n mapping	0.7650	0.4514	0.5678
	m-n mapping	-	-	-
SYN_HMM	1-1 mapping	0.8031	0.9720	0.8795
	1-n mapping	0.7413	0.4018	0.5212
	m-n mapping	-	-	-
PIALIGN(→)	1-1 mapping	0.9245	0.9444	0.9343
	1-n mapping	0.8303	0.8102	0.8201
	m-n mapping	0.0619	0.0538	0.0576
PIALIGN(←)	1-1 mapping	0.9253	0.9412	0.9331
	1-n mapping	0.8356	0.8125	0.8239
	m-n mapping	0.0600	0.0538	0.0567
Moses_grow	1-1 mapping	0.9078	0.9802	**0.9426**
	1-n mapping	0.8843	0.7927	0.8360
	m-n mapping	0.1028	0.0032	0.0063
Ours	1-1 mapping	0.9652	0.8980	0.9304
	1-n mapping	0.8579	0.8371	**0.8477**
	m-n mapping	0.2241	0.3498	**0.2732**

Table 8: Alignment performance for the different mapping case (1-1 mapping accounts for 71.87%,1-n mapping accounts for 25.55%, m-n mapping accounts for 2.58%) for Wikipedia corpora between Chinese Mainland and Hong Kong, and "-" stands for 0.

GIZA++ (Och and Ney, 2003) and Moses (Koehn et al., 2007) with union, intersecct, grow, grow-final, grow-diag, grow-diag-final, and grow-diag-final-and parameters for harmonizing the GIZA++ 1-n and m-1 alignment to m-n alignment. Meanwhile, we employ Stanford parser[10] to generate constituent parser tree for the SYN_HMM-based model. Besides, we also verify the word alignment direction for the GIZA++ and PIALIGN.

6.2 Experiment Results

In this section, we report the experiment results for the different word segmentation pairs and the all sentence pairs accordingly.

6.2.1 The Alignment Performance for the Different Word Segmentation Pairs

Table 6 shows the alignment performance for the different word segmentation pairs. In Table 6, "→" refers to the direction from HK/TW to ML, while "←" stands for the direction from ML to HK/TW instead. As it is shown, our rule-based system significantly outperforms the HMM-based, SYN_HMM-based, GIZA++ and PIALIGN systems under the two different corpus with p<0.01 using paired t-test for significance.

The best parameter for the alignment performance of Moses is grow, marking with Moses_grow in Table 6. We don't list other parameter's performance of Moses for the limited space consideration. As shown, our simple method is comparable with Moses_grow under wikipedia corpus. But our system also significantly outperforms the Moses_grow system under News corpus. The reasons are two-fold. The first reason is that the strictness characteristic of the News website, while the looseness property of the Wikipedia. The second reason is that the Moses_grow adopts many heuristic rules to improve its recall. This will be one of our future works.

Besides, these existing word alignment models are designed for the bilingual word alignment case where the order difference of the word alignment is very big. While for monolingual word alignment case, the order of the word alignment is not big enough. By comparison, our rule-based system outperforms the sophisticated HMM-based,

[10] http://nlp.stanford.edu/software/lex-parser.shtml

SYN_HMM-based, GIZA++ and PIALIGN systems because we carefully explore the characteristics of the monolingual word alignment, such as 1-1, 1-n and m-n mapping cases.

6.2.2 The Alignment Performance for the All Sentence Pairs

Table 7 shows the similar performance comparation for the all sentence pairs. The reason is similar to the description in Section 6.2.1.

Therefore, to summarize, the advantage of our model is attributed to our model can effectively extract the whole 1-n and m-n mapping cases for the monolingual word alignment corpus does not have any distorted alignment. As it is shown in Table 8, our model outperforms the GIZA++, HMM-based, SYN_HMM-based and PIALIGN modes under all mapping cases. From the recall of the 1-1 mapping case, we can know that the GIZA++ treat the majority of word alignment as 1-1 mapping, which is same as HMM-based and SYN_HMM-based models. Besides, our model can handle m-n mapping case effectively.

According to Table 6, Table 7 and Table 8, we observe that the performance of GIZA++ and PIALIGN with direction "→" outperforms the direction "←". The reason is that the granularity of word segmentation for the sentence for the HK or TW are greater than ML. Besides, the baseline of Moses with grow parameter coordinates the GIZA++ 1-n and m-1 alignment to m-n alignment with further performance improvement. It improves its recall through incorporating many heuristic rules.

7 Conclusion

In this paper, we have presented a 11,623-triple Greater China Region (GCR) word dictionary corpus and 12,000 sentence pairs GCR word alignment corpus from Wikipedia and news website, respectively. To the best of our knowledge, this is the first work to present the monolingual word alignment corpora for the GCR or three different Mandarin dialects.

Actually, our corpora may be used as a linguistic resources to test whether automatic mining of Mandarin words across different regions. Or, it may be used as a resource to transliterate between simplified and traditional variant of Mandarin. Our model explores the different word alignment case, e.g. 1-1, 1-n and m-n mapping, from Mainland China to Hong Kong or Taiwan. Evaluation results on our two different GCR word alignment corpora verify our mode can effectively deals with 1-n mapping and m-n mapping case while the-state-of-art models cannot.

In the future, we plan to expand the current two GCR corpora for the Singaporean Chinese texts use the different written variety of Chinese, together with enlarging the scale of the corpus annotation and the performance of the model.

Acknowledgments

The authors would like to thank the anonymous reviewers for their comments on this paper. This research was supported by the Research Project of State Language Commission under Grant No. YB125-99, the National Natural Science Foundation of China under Grant No. 61402208, No. 61462045 and No. 61462044, and the Natural Science Foundation of Jiangxi Province under Grant No. 20151BAB207027 and 20151BAB207025.

Reference

Necip Fazil Ayan and Bonnie J Dorr. 2006. Going beyond aer: An extensive analysis of word alignments and their impact on mt. In *Proceedings of the 21st International Conference on Computational Linguistics and the 44th annual Meeting of the Association for Computational Linguistics*, pages 9-16.

Phil Blunsom and Trevor Cohn. 2006. Discriminative Word Alignment with Conditional Random Fields. In *Proceedings of the 21st International Conference on Computational Linguistics and 44th Annual Meeting of the Association for Computational Linguistics*, pages 65-72.

Peter F Brown, Vincent J Della Pietra, Stephen A Della Pietra, and Robert L Mercer. 1993. The mathematics of statistical machine translation: Parameter estimation. *Computational Linguistics*, 19(2):263-311.

Yin-Wen Chang, Alexander M.Rush, John DeNero, and Michael Collins. 2014. A Constrained Viterbi Relaxation for Bidirectional Word Alignment. In *Proceedings of the 52nd Annual Meeting of the Association for Computational Linguistics*, pages 1481-1490.

John DeNero and Dan Klein. 2007. TailoringWord Alignments to Syntactic Machine Translation. In *Proceedings of the 45th Anfnual Meeting of the Association of Computational Linguistics*, pages 17–24.

John DeNero and Klaus Macherey. 2011. Model-based aligner combination using dual decomposition. In *Proceedings of the 49th Annual Meeting of the Association for Computational Linguistics: Human Language Technologies*, pages 420-429.

Franz Josef Och and Hermann Ney. 2003. A Systematic Comparison of Various Statistical Alignment Models. *Computational Linguistics*, 29:19-51.

Philipp Koehn, Hieu Hoang, Alexandra Birch, Chris Callison-Burch, Marcello Federico, Nicola Bertoldi, Brooke Cowan, Wade Shen, Christine Moran, Richard Zens, Chris Dyer, Ondrej Bojar, Alexandra Constantin, and Evan Herbst. 2007. Moses: Open Source Toolkit for Statistical Machine Translation, *In Proceedings of the 45th Annual Meeting of the Association for Computational Linguistics, demonstration session*, pages 177-180.

Shuhei Kondo, Kevin Duch, and Yuji Matsumoto. 2013. Hidden Markov Tree Model for Word Alignment. In *Proceedings of the Eighth Workshop on Statistical Machine Translation*, pages 503-511.

Percy Liang, Ben Taskar, and Dan Klein. 2006. Alignment by Agreement. In *Proceedings of the Human Language Technology Conference of the North American Chapter of the ACL*, pages 104–111.

Rada Mihalcea and Ted Pedersen. 2003. An Evaluation Exercise for Word Alignment. In *Proceedings of the HLT-NAACL 2003 Workshop on Building and Using Parallel Texts: Data Driven Machine Translation and Beyond*, pages 1-10.

Robert C. Moore. 2005. A Discriminative Framework for Bilingual Word Alignment. In *Proceedings of Human Language Technology Conference and Conference on Empirical Methods in Natural Language Processing*, pages 81-88.

Graham Neubig, TaroWatanabe, Eiichiro Sumita, Shinsuke Mori, Tatsuya Kawahara. 2011. An Unsupervised Model for Joint Phrase Alignment and Extraction. In *Proceedings of the 49th Annual Meeting of the Association for Computational Linguistics*, pages 632-641.

Theerawat Songyot and David Chiang. 2014. Improving Word Alignment using Word Similarity. In *Proceedings of the 2014 Conference on Empirical Methods in Natural Language Processing (EMNLP)*, pages 1840-1845.

Toshiyuki Takezawa, Eiichiro Sumita, Fumiaki Sugaya, Hirofumi Yamamoto, and Seiichi Yamamoto. 2002. Toward a Broad-coverage Bilingual Corpus for Speech Translation of Travel Conversations in the Real World. In *Proceedings of the 3rd International Conference on Language Resources and Evaluation*, pages 147-152.

Akihiro Tamura, Taro Watanabe, and Eiichiro Sumita. 2014. Recurrent Neural Networks for Word Alignment Model. In *Proceedings of the 52nd Annual Meeting of the Association for Computational Linguistics*, pages 1470-1480.

Ben Taskar, Simon Lacoste-Julien, and Dan Klein. 2005. A Discriminative Matching Approach to Word Alignment. In *Proceedings of Human Language Technology Conference and Conference on Empirical Methods in Natural Language Processing*, pages 73-80.

Chvatal Václáv, Sankoff David. 1975. "Longest common subsequences of two random sequences", *Journal of Applied Probability*, 12: 306–315.

Stephan Vogel, Hermann Ney, and Christoph Tillmann. 1996. Hmm-based word alignment in statistical translation. In *Proceedings of the 16th conference on Computational linguistics-Volume 2*, pages 836-841.

Nan Yang, Shujie Liu, Ming Zhou, and Nenghai Yu. 2013. Word Alignment Modeling with Context Dependent Deep Neural Network. In *Proceedings of the 51st Annual Meetings of the Association for Computational Linguistics*, pages 166-175.

Author Index

Ács, Judit, 73

Bick, Eckhard, 34
Bobicev, Victoria, 59

Costa, Hernani, 66

Derczynski, Leon, 10
Dras, Mark, 35

Ezeani, Ignatius, 24

Fabra Boluda, Raül, 52
Franco-Salvador, Marc, 11

Gebre, Binyam Gebrekidan, 66
Goutte, Cyril, 78
Grad-Gyenge, László, 73

Hepple, Mark, 24

Jauhiainen, Heidi, 44
Jauhiainen, Tommi, 44

Kumar, Arun, 17

Leger, Serge, 78
Li, Maoxi, 85
Lindén, Krister, 44
Ljubešić, Nikola, 1

Malmasi, Shervin, 35

Nakov, Preslav, 1

Oliver, Antoni, 17
Onyenwe, Ikechukwu, 24

Padró, Lluís, 17

Rangel, Francisco, 11, 52
Rodrigues de Rezende Oliveira, Thiago Bruno, 73
Rosso, Paolo, 11, 52

Tan, Liling, 1
Tiedemann, Jörg, 1

Uchechukwu, Chinedu, 24

van Genabith, Josef, 66

Wang, Mingwen, 85

xu, fan, 85
Xu, Xiongfei, 85

Zampieri, Marcos, 1, 66